D. F. CAPSTONE

HOW TO BE MORE MINDFUL AND MEDITATE

The quickest path to be more present with a deeper connection

First edition

This book was professionally typeset on Reedsy.
Find out more at reedsy.com

To my three beautiful daughters.
I know this book will help you one day.
For I love you all more than you will ever know...

To the mind that is still, the whole universe surrenders.

Lao Tzu

Contents

1

Introduction: Unlocking the Secrets of Inner Peace

How are you going?

David is my name.

Let me say how grateful I am that you've taken the plunge to read this book.

I am so excited to be able to work with you closely and help you through the chapters ahead. I have a lot of great things to share with you that will benefit you immensely if you choose to take them on board and put the theory to practice.

My personal life has been a massive journey.

One in which I was put in a difficult position which forced me to dig deep and enter a path to self-mastery. Nonetheless, this was an incredible phase of my life, which has made me the man I am today.

This book isn't about me, though; this book is about you. You have your own story. There is a reason you've clicked on this book to purchase it. When you think about understanding mindfulness and meditation, what is it you want to gain within yourself and see happen?

Mindfulness and meditation is such a fascinating topic as it has this hidden mystery to it. That unknown element drawing you in wanting to know more. Then, whenever you hear someone speaking about it that meditates regularly, you hear them speaking swearing by it with their whole heart. That look in their eyes, you know it's real, like they have found something magical within them.

Nonetheless, for me, the hardest thing I found, was that every book I tried reading, every video I tried watching, every course I looked into, didn't explain it clearly enough. Either that or I couldn't resonate or connect with the way they were explaining it.

Have you found this yourself?

If this is the first book you've clicked on for this topic, then I say you are truly blessed to find this one straight away. I hope to save you many, many hours.

So many people fail to realize just how much the mind blocks us from truly seeing life. We've just learned to accept it, yapping away at us, trying to do everything in its power to keep our focus on it, and that's why I say, two hands down, that having mental clarity and emotional mastery is the most important gift one could ask for, hence, why I say with a smile of confidence, that this book is life-changing.

For me, being able to stop and see those little jewels life presents to us daily, is the thing that means the most.

If you are seeking this, I know you are going to love this book. The keys I will be sharing with you, will allow you to keep your thoughts and feelings in control. It will also provide you with a greater connection to life from moment to moment, seeing it for what it is.

Let us begin this walk together as I show you what I mean.

Lets get into it

I have written this book to have several layers to it.

You can either treat this book as merely a feel-good read, taking in a pearl or two as you read through it, then bring those pearls into your world to help you break through those blocks that may be holding you back. The second layer, which I would recommend, is a little deeper. That is to treat this book more as a hands-on workshop: applying the keys I release through each chapter, then run through each reflection and meditation I share through each chapter, to ensure that everything I share with you stays with you to help you witness this profound change within yourself.

The third and fourth layers are when you revisit this book in the coming months to recharge yourself, reflecting on what changes you may or may not have introduced, bring yourself back on track, and integrate another layer of self-mastery into your world.

I have congested this book purposely to give any reader so many things to work towards and to make sure that the second read is even better than the first.

If you dive in deep the first time you're reading this, following the instructions I give, you will have a much deeper experience reading this. This in itself, will take you so much further within yourself.

If you are just enjoying reading it so much and start binge reading, that's also okay. Just try to do at least one reflection and meditation exercise a day in the sequence I have given from the date you started reading. This will make sure you walk away from this book understanding how to meditate and are living a little more mindfully, for that's why you've purchased the book right?

A couple of ground rules

Firstly, let me be clear: this book does not discuss religion. I believe there's a universal truth behind every religion, but this book goes beyond religion.

This book is designed to help you find and hold a constant connection to life and everything around you.

Whatever faith you follow, that is your personal journey and I respect it entirely. Nonetheless, I have written this book with intent that anyone on the planet can pick it up and read it, so I can then show them how to slow down to the speed of life and become constantly mindful. Which, to those of you who are religious, will unquestionably help you see God more continually in action around you.

Anyone reading this that isn't religious, I am grateful you are reading this. Please know that if you take on the suggestions I give throughout this book and make them your own, you will bring so much more joy into your world. You will find the simplest things around you then lightening up your day, which, as a result, will lift those around you as well. Your sense of life will deepen in so many ways.

This book is designed to be a practical tool for anyone who picks it up, regardless of whether it is today or in the years to come.

I have written this book in a way that will reach everyone.

I will mention, though, that this is a book about meditation and mindfulness There are certain elements of this topic where I have to explain spiritual elements within my words. However, my focus has been on explaining everything as neutral as

4

possible.

I must point out, too, that I am sharing a lot of things that have opened up to me personally as I have pursued meditating and entering those higher states of consciousness. I will say, that everyone is unique, and your internal experiences may be completely different to mine. If none of my shared experiences or perspectives align to you, please see it as an exercise to help you stretch your creative imagination of where you can take this once you finish this book. I ask you to follow through my guidance through the path I am weaving, as the goal of this book is to take you as high as I can and help you find your inner self. From there, you will have your inner self or intuition guiding you.

This is my reason for writing this book, and I share it openly.

However, I will also be clearly explaining how to self correct every element of a busy mind, still your thoughts, then approach meditation practically, guiding you through how to meditate correctly, then introduce you to mindfulness, giving you a deeper understanding of universal love which will bring you into a divine romance with life.

There is so much more within the pages ahead, this is just to list a few things of what to expect from reading this, so even if you don't connect with your inner self the first time reading, you will still see so much change in your life after absorbing what I am about to share with you.

If you read this more than once it will be a totally different experience.

The keys within this book will help anyone who reads it become the best version of themselves in how they live and experience life.

This book focuses on increasing your awareness and self-mastery. For, the more transparent the windows are to your being, the more you will see in life.

Please, though, be open to my suggestions. As there may be thirty things I say for example, that you disagree with, still, if there is even one key you hear from my words and practice integrating into your life, that then becomes a daily habit, and starts changing your life for the better, isn't that a victory for both of us?

- You have to be open and listening, though.
- We never stop learning as long as we are open and receptive to hearing and finding new things.
- The moment we stop learning, we stop living.

Remember that.

Also, through this book, I speak a lot about love. The love I am referring to is not a relationship love, where you heart reacts to being in someone else's company.

The same love we have all been lead to believe is the only way to happiness...

Nonsense!

This love I am speaking of, is more when we begin emanating our creative energies within our emotions to the correct vibration leading us to start swimming more with the waves of life.

However, if you can't feel the love pouring out of your being at the intensity that I am speaking of, please know that if your mind is still and you are at peace in your feeling world, that peace you are feeling comes from love.

Once we start feeling the harmony in aligning ourselves with life, all of a sudden, the doors open for us, and we begin entering deeper and deeper into more profound levels of unconditional love.

Let's begin by working on attuning to feeling at peace and putting that feeling into our being as we go through the exercises in the book. By doing that, the moments we experience will gradually increase in intensity. Then, we will start feeling the waters of love filling our hearts to the point where we can begin letting it flow into our worlds more constantly.

Understanding your 'Why'?

The fact you have purchased this book and are reading or listening to it tells me you want to learn and grow as a person. It could be your soul searching, seeking peace or more control within yourself, or maybe looking for something more...

It could be all those things.

I know it was for me.

The biggest key is to find your goal or list of goals you want to achieve from reading this book, write them down on paper or on n your phones notes, and revisit them while you read. It also keeps those goals at the forefront of your mind as you reflect on all the suggested changes through the chapters ahead.

Experience has taught me that it is only when you start putting things to paper that they start becoming real.

- It might be something as simple as wanting to still your emotions to the anxiety you often wrestle with.
- Or being able to switch off from work when you get home at night to be more present and connected with your children.
- Or maybe you want to build a habit of practicing medi-

7

tation, but haven't found the correct answer or the right teacher.

I've written this book intending to help resolve all these things.

The answer you are looking for is coming...

And if you have no motive or goals and can't find the fuel to your fire, that is also okay. However, everyone has at least a few things they need to work on, and if you think you don't, I say you are blinded by your own pride and need to work on that before you can start seeing what's really going on.

We all have those moments occasionally where we lose our cool, overreact, or even wind ourselves up while functioning in the world or interacting with others.

- Imagine if you never lost your harmony and overreacted last year, and in that one year, if you'd be in a different place to where you are now.
- Imagine living life for the next twenty, thirty, forty years from now, being a better person, connected, and present to everyone around you and how much more impact you'd have to those around you.
- Imagine the impact you'd leave on those you truly love and how they would see you as a person.
- Imagine, then, in your later years in life, old and grey, sitting back and reflecting on it all and being able to reflect on everything you had done and what you gave back to life.

Okay, now let's say you did nothing to better yourself, accepting the flaws you have, then put both possible timelines next to each other, both of you did something about it and if you didn't.

Imagine now, if you just made even one slight change within yourself, such as taking a breath before responding to a heated conversation. This, in turn, helped extend the years of your marriage, or helped the way you responded in parenting, thus, increasing your child's self-esteem, which then helps drive them to succeed and climb further in life, and they, in time, treat their children the same way you had treated them, mirroring the way they were raised growing up.

Regardless if you are married or have children, can you start to see how much impact we currently on those around us?

Now start to picture the type of effect that making even small changes could have on your career and life opportunities in the coming years.

I may ruffle some feathers here for a moment but, let's look back at how you've handled yourself through life on a day-to-day basis for a second: with your partner, your family, your children, your work colleagues, and your friends...

Do you think in hindsight you could have done anything better?

We can't change the past, but by being present we can change the future.

If you never engaged in fear, anxiety, or anger, I am sure every interaction to life would be steering in your favor.

I may have touched some sensitive memories and moments with some of you reading, I apologize, please stay with me, there is a reason for that reflective exercise.

I've taken you through these reflective questions to prompt you to face those parts of yourself that very few people want to look at.

Ignorance is bliss.

Sometimes, we have to let the feeling of pain outweigh the easier option to do nothing which gives us a driving force to take action and take that first step.

The reflection exercises explained

At the end of each chapter, I will present a reflection exercise on the lesson theme of the chapter.

Please complete every one of them in the sequence of the chapters. Every one of them plays a part to the ultimate end result, which is, you being able to live life in the moment, free from thought and unnecessary emotion.

With some exercises, I will ask you to grab a pen and paper. You'll benefit greatly by doing so. However, if you don't have a pen or paper, you can open up notes and type them on your phone or do the reflective exercise later on, but don't forget to do them!

If you are just reading through, try to pause for at least 15 to 20 seconds on each question I give and reflect on it at least, as it will force things to surface in you to allow you to self-reflect more and grow through the exercises. Some of the other reflections will be more of a physical activity or mindful meditation. Every reflective exercise plays its part in giving you more clarity on something or investigating the chapters theme. This will ultimately help you retain and absorb the lesson just shared as well.

The meditation exercises explained

Each chapter will also contain a different meditation exercise to help you in your day-to-day life. I trust they will serve you well. Within these pages, there is an alchemy; you'll either find it, or it will find you if you follow every chapter as I have suggested. You may also journal your experiences on paper after the reflections and meditations, although that is optional.

Rather than having you sit in some lotus position for hours on end next to a moss rock waterfall, the meditations I have included are very simple and designed to be both a combination of active and practical meditations so that you can integrate them into your day-to-day life and at any time of the day.

When I say an active meditation, I mean a meditation that can be given throughout the day while working or shopping for example.

The ultimate aim is not to just be meditating and resetting once in the morning, but constantly throughout the day. That way we can close the gaps of the busy mind resurfacing so we can stay in a space of peace more constantly.

All of the meditations can be given independently, or they can also be blended and merged together as you progress through the book. I am your teacher now, As you are reading this book and we work together, I ask you to follow the meditations I suggest. There is a reason for this, which you'll find for yourself shortly. The ultimate key is going within so we can raise in consciousness and connect with our inner self. I have mapped out each meditation specifically to help you achieve this for yourself so long as you follow my guidance.

Once you finish this book, you should be able to meditate comfortably, conquer your monkey mind, and be able to slow down your thoughts and feelings at any time effortlessly while living your life constantly in a similar state to meditation.

If you take my hand and trust the process, you'll gain so

much from this book.

Reflection exercise: visualize your future self

Here we are, your first reflection exercise. Take a minute to grab your pen and paper if you can. If you have ever attended a seminar or workshop to better yourself, it is quite common to have a short goal-setting exercise at the start and reflective questions throughout the seminar where you are forced to face yourself, reflecting on what you have just learned, and how you can apply these ideas into your world.

This book is a book on meditation and mindfulness, let us look at your why...

Let me start with why did you buy this book?

In the perfect world, if this book helped you answer everything and resolved every problem you are wrestling with, how would you feel?

What would this version of you look like?

As you hold that picture of your perfect outcome and that version of yourself you are looking to become, let us jot down some notes and reflect on some questions. Grab your phone out if you don't have a pen and paper.

Don't be scared to start writing, watch how much your reflective answers will then guide you in finding the answers you are looking for.

Okay, you ready? First question, what do you want to achieve from this book?

You bought this book for a reason, what was it?

Spend some time jotting down what you want to achieve, even if it's twenty different points, and get it out of your head and into the physical plane.

Okay, now let's go through these next questions:

- What would you change in your world right now?
- What changes would you want to see in yourself?

Imagine when all these changes came to be and what your future self would look like...

- How would you act?
- How would you feel?
- What would others think of you and see in you when in your company?

Keep visualizing this version of yourself in the future once you achieved all these goals. I want you to hold this in your mind now for a minute. Close your eyes for five to ten seconds and try to paint this image of your future self vividly.

What you see, that you'll manifest.

That vision you've just seen in your mind, throughout the rest of this book I want you to hold that vision of yourself...

This is now you.

This is who you want to become.

Your goal has become my goal now too. remember that as we continue working together.

All that separates you from this is time now...

So throughout the book, as I share keys with you and we progress together, this version you've painted in inner vision, let's make it happen.

You've already created it within your mind, now it's just a matter of the outer self adjusting. This reflective exercise is more than setting goals, remember to hold this vision of yourself while reading through the chapters ahead.

Meditation exercise. three breaths to freedom

This first meditation is an active meditation, meaning it can be given at any time. You can give this whenever you want throughout the day, so if you ever feel out of sorts, try it. Rather than getting you to close your eyes and chant the Ommm straight away, building a little momentum of being able to still your thoughts and settle your feelings with your breath is an excellent starting point. This will be yours to use if you are struggling at all with the more advanced meditations in the chapters ahead, if you ever drift off wandering in thought or feel discomfort, by simply focusing on and listening to your breath, you will be able to steer your ship back to meditating and continue going deeper...

It is short and sweet, but surprisingly invigorating. It can also be given in public when people are next to you and they wouldn't even know. Say if you were in a waiting room, in class, or at your work desk.

The first time we give this, I would like you to be sitting down. It doesn't matter which hand you choose; I'd like you to tap your hand or finger on something to the count of a metronome. You could be tapping your leg, your work desk, the arm of a couch, or even your thumb and middle finger together. We will use this counting from the tapping to breathe to the rhythm of eight.

Meaning:

- Eight seconds of breathing in through your nose.
- Eight seconds holding your breath.
- Eight seconds, breathing out through your mouth.
- Eight seconds of holding our breath, then repeating the cycle again.

This means you should be tapping 96 times minimum. Once ready and in position, close your eyes and:

- Breathe in for the first eight counts.
- Hold your breath in and continue to tap for the following eight counts.
- Breathe out, still tapping for the following eight counts.
- Continue tapping while refraining from breathing for the following eight counts.

Once you finish the three rounds of breathing, open your eyes again.

You should feel lighter and more invigorated.

This is just a quick and easy meditation designed to be the ace up your sleeve to pull out in times of need, short and sharp for when we need it most.

Things to consider

Seeing an image of your future self is crucial with the way

I have composed this book. This is not just a book about meditation. Once we cover meditation, we'll be entering the most immense levels of mindfulness and striving to stay in that state constantly. With your future self visualized, once you see you fall off course, or get distracted, within one or two breaths and reconnecting, we are back on course. It's just a matter of closing those gaps where we fall back into our old ways quicker and return back to being connected to everything.

I have always known by writing out our goals on paper, they have a greater chance of being achieved, versus holding them in our heads, which means it's still all fantasy. There is something about goal setting; meaning once you put it on paper, it becomes real, like it's the first step to manifesting something.

This three-breaths to freedom technique will help you throughout your days, at least for the start of this book.

Your possibly grunting to yourself now, "I'm paying all this money and he's teaching me how to breath!"

You should know, I don't give away any of my good stuff in the Kindle preview ;)

Nonetheless, once you learn and have built momentum with this three-breath-to-freedom exercise, you can use this technique anytime.

You can experiment with tapping your thumb against your middle finger softly while walking around at work.

You can tap your thumb on the shopping trolley handle while you're walking down the aisles of a supermarket.

You can also give it while you're briskly walking. If you step fast enough, you can use your footsteps to do the counting. If your constant with it, watch how many things you get done within an hour or two.

This meditation is also powerful for anyone wrestling with anxiety. The breath moves the tension from the body, providing you are breathing from your diaphragm, which takes a little practice of pushing your stomach out as you breathe in through your nose. This makes sure you are filling the bottom two-thirds of your lungs with fresh air and energy. What I mean is try pushing out your stomach like you've overeaten, and your belly is popping out while you breathe in.

I will cover this breathing practice a little deeper in a later chapter.

As simple as this meditation sounds, with all the other tools I will share in later chapters, this breathing exercise here will help bring you back into alignment almost instantly, especially while out in public and around others.

2

Reboot Your Mind: Clearing the Clutter

I often hear people claiming they can multitask and how efficient it makes them, but we also need to realize that as soon as our minds are pointed in more than one direction, they struggle.

Yes, we can do it, and we can do it easily. The problem with multitasking and operating with our minds juggling multiple tasks at once is it clouds our creative genius from shining through.

With our minds active all the time, it's like we are running our hands through the water in a fish pond; all the dirt rises, making it muddy and cloudy. It's not till you pull back that the mud settles, and you can see through the water again. A still mind gives us a more transparent window into more visions and insight into our creativity and problem-solving.

Not to mention that once we start setting our mind tasks to complete and fail to complete them, the tasks start building up like bricks in a backpack, sitting on the back burner of our brain. We need to realize the amount of weight we begin to carry around. What's worse, we often forget many of the tasks, and it's not until we start to switch off at night that our brain wants to shut down, and it starts reminding us of the tasks we need to complete to try and let go.

Quite often, what spirals from here is that we begin to negatively judge ourselves with condemnation because we forgot to complete those tasks and end up laying in bed with thoughts circling around our minds like a washing machine. It's a vicious cycle; there has got to be a better method to manage our days.

Clearing your desktop

There is a hack around this, you know.

You need to sit down and start jotting down all the tasks and every commitment you have made to yourself on paper.

- I am talking about every chore you know needs doing around the house. This includes that thing outside that needs fixing or the paint chipping away in the laundry (to give examples).
- I am talking about the tasks you've taken recently or set yourself at work.
- I am talking about your personal goals.
- I am talking about the tasks you've set yourself for the people you know you need to call or go see.

Take the time and start jotting them down one by one on paper or in your notes app on your phone. By writing it down, your mind can finally let go from holding the command you gave to be a reminder system, as it knows you now have it in front of you on paper.

Once you start getting through all of the commitments and things you've set yourself to do this week, getting them on paper, lo and behold, last week's commitments start surfacing. It's almost as if your mind is operating like a desktop, with all these tabs open, but you can't see them because you have more recent windows open in front of the original tasks

Once you get every tab open or task you've set yourself from out of your head and onto paper, this feeling is linked to it.

To me, it's similar to feeling endorphins after training. Your mind feels like it's finally been able to drop its workload. You feel clarity. You can function and operate so much easier mentally and creatively.

This is an excellent feeling.

We should constantly feel and be operating like this.

You could run through this exercise at least once a month for the next couple of months and see if it works for you.

As we move forward, if this makes sense to you and you desire to avoid putting that workload on your mind so much, try to build the habit of having a to-do list that you fill out at night before bed so that when you start the day, you have a system in place to crush it productively. You also free your mind from having to be a constant reminder system, exhausting yourself mentally trying to juggle your daily tasks in your mind while working on completing them.

Your to-do list is either in the notes on your phone, a small pad on your desk, or even a post-it note at work. You look at the first task, smash through it and complete it, line it out on your list or tick it, and move on to the next one.

You may get caught off guard and distracted at times, but one thought to prompt you to bring your focus on your to-do list, and you've closed the gap and your back on point.

Operating like this gives you a compass to guide you through your days, instead of living life lost at sea.

It also gives your mind a greater focus and clarity, rather than operating like you've just thrown a rock at a beehive.

Revisiting your to-do list daily is vital.

At night works best for me; some people would rather do it first thing in the morning. When I go to bed, though, with my list of tasks for tomorrow already on paper, there is an added layer of focus, like it's ingrained in my unconscious. You wake up focused on completing as much as possible.

When you revisit your list, see what you have done and haven't. Then, bring those uncompleted tasks onto tomorrow's list with your new tasks as you start scheduling tomorrow. It takes a bit of practice, but it is the practice that makes us professionals.

What is distracting you right now?

To understand ourselves, we need to be aware at least of everything and every force that is distracting us from holding attention to ourselves. And your number one kryptonite Superman, sucking away your focus and power right now, is in your pocket.

It's your smart phone.

All the notifications, apps, and doom scrolling...

Can you wait in line for a coffee or meal, stand in a lift, hop into bed, or sit through a lunch break without checking your phone and running your finger or thumb on the touch screen for comfort?

Relax; I ain't your papa.

I am only asking you to try and minimize it a little or at least be mindful of it when you catch yourself scrolling, so you are no longer a slave and ignorant to the algorithms of the hive mind.

You also have a TV trying to distract you. Friends or family members are calling you on the phone for a feel-good conversation, pulling you in a different direction, and stealing your time.

Let's not forget marketing everywhere, bombarding you from every angle on billboards as you drive in your car to and from work every day.

The algorithms of your social media, squeezing in sponsored posts and ads in every space possible, trying to do anything it can to turn you into a cash cow.

This and so much more, feeding your monkey mind bananas from every direction.

There are definitely a lot of forces at play.

Don't worry, there is a solution, and it's within yourself.

As you become more heart-centered, these things out there will still be doing their thing, bombarding you. You'll just be like a pillar of fire, unshakable and anchored, internally focusing on more important things than the temporal exterior gains around you.

Reflection exercise: free your mind

Earlier in the chapter, I spoke about freeing your mind from the commitments you have made to yourself and all the tasks you carry around like baggage in the back of your mind.

Let's grab that notebook and start writing out all the tasks we have set for ourselves today:

- Write them out individually, then start thinking about the chores you need to do around your house or someone elses, and get them on paper.
- Then, think of the tasks you must do at work and get them all on paper.
- That business idea or project you have planned and set a list of tasks to complete, get it on paper.
- That friend you were supposed to call who you haven't spoken to in ages—get it on paper.
- Bring any personal tasks, such as fitness or relationship goals, onto paper.
- Did you ever plan to build the kids a cubby house outside or any other Sunday projects? Get it on paper.

Get every task on paper and watch the commitments you completely forgot about, start surfacing. These can continue going back for weeks, even months. Once you get them all out on paper, keep it to the side of your bed or desk and observe the shift in yourself and how much easier it is to keep what you need to do on that piece of paper than to hold everything in your mind.

I know which one I prefer out of the two.

Meditation exercise: listening gracefully

In today's meditation exercise, we will work on developing an active meditation you can start doing at any time of the day if you're feeling out of sorts.

Learning the secret to what happens when you 'listen gracefully' and observe the audio around you will serve you in so many ways. This is the easiest and fastest way to empty yourself, leading you through the doorway into mindfulness. It will also help you in the future with the more advanced meditations I'll be sharing with you in the chapters ahead. You can do this all day and every day if you really pursue it.

Once you learn and understand that the quickest way to overcome anxiety or keep your mind from racing thoughts in to just stop and listen, with no opinion or self-talk categorizing what's happening, nothing but observing and searching for sounds around you.

Then, keep listening until you break through and feel comfortable and at peace.

Once you are comfortable emptying your mind to listen, every sound you search for becomes more and more rewarding, like you are entering deeper and deeper into living with an empty mind.

People meditate for hours to empty their minds, yet at any time, if we just listen, we are able to actively bring ourselves into a similar state.

You will become less and less rattled by the feelings of anxiety or racing thoughts if you do this exercise constantly.

This will give you so much more control in life.

It takes a little practice, though. So let's practice.

Let us go outside somewhere, preferably with nature.

If you are in a dense city with cars and traffic, that is okay, as long as you can hear random ambient sounds around you.

Take a seat and sit comfortably; now, close your eyes and listen. If thoughts arise, breathe them in and out and keep listening. It can be uncomfortable initially when we close our eyes as we start facing discomfort within our subconscious.

If you encounter any discomfort, keep listening and searching for sounds around you.

Visualize that your ears are like the radars you see in the submarines and boats, if that helps.

What can you hear?

Listen gracefully...

Think of a captivated child looking towards a mound of ants, entirely at the moment, and not worrying about a thing.

As you continue to listen, there is something you are listening for...

It is the sound behind the sounds you are hearing.

The sound of silence. They say it's silence, but it isn't silence at all.

As soon as we hear the sound of silence, and start listening into the sound of silence for more sounds, our consciousness starts expanding.

Yet, very few people have witnessed this and can sit comfortably in silence.

Why is that?

What is stopping them?

Who really cares right now? Just keep listening gracefully, waiting for the sounds as you enter deeper and deeper into what should feel like a childlike joy.

This joy is a gift.

A limitless gift.

After you have completed this task, I want you to set an alarm on your phone three times throughout the day tomorrow at different times.

For example, at 10:30 am, 2:00 pm, and 5:00 pm, then once that alarm goes off, take a minute or two to empty your mind by listening to the sounds of what is happening around you.

You can do this at work or any time because we are only focusing on listening, which isn't hurting anyone.

If any thought comes to mind, that's okay; acknowledge it, keep listening, and keep going until you break through to that feeling of peace. Keep focusing on listening until you slow your mind and settle your emotions.

After breaking through to peace with this trick a couple of times, you'll never feel powerless to a racing mind or uncomfortable emotions because you'll know how to pull yourself out of it by only listening.

Listening gracefully in this way can become quite addictive, as it constantly draws you into a better space and takes you deeper and deeper into these comfortably intense levels of emptiness.

You hear everything when people communicate with you, and you are listening like this. You also see the situation perfectly because the desktop is clear. Then, when you speak, your words have wisdom.

Things to consider

The key to meditation is understanding that it involves emptying our minds and returning to our native state. While we are out in the world, though, it's hard to say to our partner or work colleague, *"Hang on, let me go away and meditate and chant the Omm to get back into sorts before we continue this conversation."*

Nonetheless, we can empty our minds on call once we have cultivated the skill of listening gracefully. Think of your mind as a see-saw with two sides of the brain. One is the active side, and the other is the observing side; the active side is problem-solving, which tries to calculate solutions, whereas the observing side is more absorbing and creative.

Most people get caught up in having the active side, trying

to run the show constantly, getting stuck in their heads, and finding themselves out of balance. Nonetheless, the quickest way to regain balance is to stop thinking, drop all opinions, and start genuinely listening with an empty mind, free of thought or distractions.

Once we let the silt of our mind settle, our intuitive wisdom in responding trickles into our being like a waterfall, and we start acting and reacting from the point of our inner self.

3

Dig Deeper: Discovering Hidden Layers of Your Being

So now, in this chapter, it's time to dig deeper. The first couple of chapters have laid the foundation; now, we can explore meditation more deeply and try to understand its true purpose.

Before we get started, though, can I ask... *"Did you do the exercises in the previous chapter?"*

"You didn't?? Well, go back and do it. I will say it again: you will get so much more from this book if you put the theory into practice."

Oh, you have done them?

Awesome! Let us carry on...

Why meditate?

So why do we meditate?

I will share my humble opinion. We meditate to quiet those external distractions and confront ourselves.

This transformative practice forces our thoughts and emotions to settle, returning us to what I will call our 'native state', which is completely thought-free, in a state of grace with a sense of expansion and peripheral awareness of everything around us.

Once we enter that native state, we feel completely comfortable. We instantly recognize it, like a part of us feels at home and wants to stay in that state for as long as possible.

Then, as we hold ourselves in that state and refrain from engaging with anything, similar to a radio station; we start tuning into the vibration that all of nature and life operate on.

Once aligned with all around you, because you are tuning into this universal vibration, you naturally begin to feel expansive and are able to expand your consciousness and awareness.

That sense of oneness, often spoken of in meditation, may be an attempt to describe the connection I speak of. Hence, I am coining the term - 'our native state.'

I believe that the ultimate purpose of meditation is to familiarize ourselves with this native state so that when we return to our daily responsibilities, we can work towards bringing that state into our daily lives.

Meditation explained

Many practices and meditation methods exist from various faiths and cultural backgrounds. I could have composed a book that explained the various techniques from these different disciplines, then let you choose your own adventure. The fact remains, though...

You have a smartphone.

We are in a Golden Age with technology at your fingertips.

This is a task you may choose to visit yourself at a later date, but again that is entirely up to you.

I believe that meditation, in all its forms, serves one common goal:

- It forces us to surrender the active world around us
- It settles our thoughts and feelings
- It reconnects us to feeling our native state
- It increases our discipline in self-mastery
- It brings us into contact with our inner self

Like jumping on the treadmill for twenty minutes to get fit; meditation makes our mind fit. It clears our thoughts. And when the mind is empty, wisdom flows.

Those jewels found through sitting in silence and facing our inner self are where we gain a greater insight into life. Often, this is the time when we are given solutions to any problems we face, which helps us take back the reins to life.

By emptying our minds and reconnecting with our native state, we align ourselves with life. The walls of separation begin to crumble as our sense of self and the division around us dissolve, and we start expanding into deeper levels of consciousness.

Mindfulness versus meditation

Meditation is how we empty ourselves, reconnect to our native state, recharging ourselves internally, and overcome all outer distraction.

Mindfulness in contrast, becomes the next step from meditation where we continue actively meditating. It's when we begin to creatively express being in that native state as we operate and function through our days.

We close our eyes in meditation and enter deeper levels of bliss in heightened consciousness so that when we open our eyes and return to our lives, we can bring that internal truth and share it with others, and transfer that feeling of harmony to everything around us.

Mindfulness is when we become completely present in every moment, experiencing it in a similar state to meditation, only it's active. It is then we see ourselves as a window, shining that light from our inner self through our actions and expressions and into every moment around us.

Benefits of meditation

Being able to wait in line for a cup of coffee by yourself and not have one thought enter your mind is an incredible life skill.

There are so many benefits to meditation. Just by meditating for even ten minutes before you start your day, you witness so many changes within yourself:

- You find yourself more focused with a clearer mind, making you more productive with your daily tasks.
- Because you've spent some time resetting into your native state, when emotions or thoughts start creeping in throughout the day, you can notice them and correct them quickly.
- You'll notice there will be little moments throughout the day that stand out to you where you are reminded of your native state or to tune back into it.
- When your head hits the pillow that night, you'll fall asleep faster as you can still your thoughts and feelings quicker

to drift off to sleep.

Most importantly, because you are continuously facing your-self, surrendering and letting go of the world around you to go within, you are bringing another level of consciousness into your world. This adds another dimension to life, giving you the ability now to start climbing higher in consciousness.

As you are constantly stilling the waters of your being until you feel at peace, you become happy within yourself. This makes you less dependent on the need for stimulation from the outer world.

Many people self-medicate themselves with distractions constantly to avoid facing themselves, as it can often be uncom-fortable for them. This no longer becomes an issue for those who meditate, as they have found peace from entering within, and everything becomes nothing more than an extension of that peace they are feeling.

The monkey mind

You may have heard the term 'the monkey mind' used before through discussions on meditation, which is a metaphor for the busy mind. It has also been labelled as the carnal mind or lesser self. The monkey mind is the busy mind, always active, trying to distract you with anything it can to try and pull you away from going within and stilling yourself.

"Does the monkey want a banana?" you ask while waving a smartphone in their face.

This monkey mind is often hard to beat when we first begin trying to meditate. At the start, it can make meditation feel quite uncomfortable. The monkey mind is actually the greatest force of opposition you will face when trying to meditate, so listen closely.

After two or three times of breaking through the grips of the monkey mind and entering into the first stages of meditation, you feel a sense of victory within yourself. Not only giving you more strength for future meditations, but also if your mind starts racing later throughout the day. We don't feel so powerless by our thoughts trying to run the show all the time because we have learned we can beat it through meditation.

Developing the ability to still your mind, cage that monkey, and keep it still is one of the first things we need to do to enable us to find our inner self.

Beat the beast

This is where we come to the point in our journey where we look to cage that monkey or slay the dragon that stands in the way of us gaining access to the kingdom of life.

But it's not too big of a challenge once we understand the process.

Just as there is a lot of pressure put on coal before it starts forming diamonds, we must go through being uncomfortable to get a little more comfortable.

I want you to think of this phase of gaining control of the mind like dealing with a spoiled little child. One that is trying everything in its power to have its way.

There are only a couple of cards it can play to try and distract you and cause you to give up trying to succeed in meditating.

As you begin trying to meditate, you may experience things like:

- A heaviness in your feelings and turbulence in your emotions, making it uncomfortable to sit with your eyes closed.
- Thoughts start popping into your mind, reminding you of everything you need to do.
- You get the feeling that this is stupid what you are trying to achieve, and you are wasting time.
- You may experience several more intrusive thoughts attempting to throw you off or pull you into distraction...

With anything that happens, just breathe in through your nose, imagining that your breath is consuming the negativity you are wrestling with, and as you breathe out, imagine your breath is releasing it and the negativity leaving you along with your breath.

Just observe what is happening and keep focusing on your breath. If you start feeling uncomfortable in your emotions, this is the last card it has to play.

Ride the wave and know you've already won.

Checkmate!

Just breathe the tension in with love and breathe it out. The monkey mind will be forced to let go, and that's when you'll enter into the first state of meditation. You should recognize the feeling instantly once you enter it.

It is a feeling of peace.

Your first couple of battles with the monkey mind may be easier than this; I'm trying to map out the process as much as possible to make everything easier for you, giving you the foresight to anticipate every challenge you could potentially face.

My heart is on you winning with this and succeeding so we

can keep moving forward.

Reflection exercise: close your eyes and face yourself

Okay, so I've talked you through the process; now, I want you to close your eyes and face your subconscious. You may have already mastered this and not have to go through the process of caging the monkey. Either way, I want you to close your eyes and still your mind.

Set a timer on your phone for at least five minutes.

Laying down, sitting in a parked car, sitting on the couch, or at your desk, it does not matter.

Five minutes of having your eyes closed and settling your mind to where it is not thinking about anything and where you feel comfortable not thinking or having thoughts with no desire to think about anything.

You will be a new person once you open your eyes again.

You should be feeling nothing but comfort being in this space with your eyes closed.

Completely comfortable.

This is your native state.

We want to feel like this all the time.

With any discomfort or tension in your thoughts or feelings you experience, use your breath to absorb them by breathing it into your heart, feeling the discomfort being transmuted, and breathing the discomfort out of your being until you are at peace and completely still.

Once you reach the state where you feel you're in a state of meditation with your mind and feeling completely silent, you can open your eyes and end the meditation.

For all those going all in with this book, you should stay

in this state a little longer, which I encourage you to do. If you choose to extend your meditation, you may want to observe your emotions and search for the hidden feelings in the background you can feel by being in your native state with your thoughts and feelings empty.

You may journal your experience after the 5 minutes is over, but again, that is optional.

Meditation exercise: the shining white pearl of the heart

This meditation exercise is one of my favorites, and one I often do in bed before drifting off to sleep at night. It's also a great one to give after getting home from work after a hard day and feeling exhausted and needing to recharge and reset.

It's an excellent meditation to do lying down, but one you can do while sitting.

Set an alarm on your phone for ten minutes.

Let us aim for a minimum of ten minutes, but if you're enjoying it and want to extend it, you can do that too.

With your middle finger, touch the center of your chest to anchor your point of focus.

Now, visualize a white translucent pearl shining brightly and filled with white fire within the center of your chest, approximately the size of a dime or small marble.

I will refer to it as a shining white pearl from here on.

With your focus on the shining white pearl, imagine your breaths breathing in, being pulled into the center of this pearl, and your breaths breathing out, coming from the center the pearl.

Any thoughts and feelings you experience surface, see them being pulled into this shining white pearl with your breaths.

Keep focusing on the white pearl and your breaths and nothing else until it becomes the center of your universe.

Feel your breath breathing in the fire and light from this shining white pearl and fanning the fire of the pearl when you breathe out.

The white fire shines bright like the midday sun shining on snow. It is diamond-white, beautiful and majestic.

Your center of awareness is entirely on this pearl within the center of your heart.

There is no outer attachment or distraction; everything except this shining white pearl fades to exist.

Continue focusing on breathing in and out its white light, but now begin feeling the white light rejuvenate your body completely.

When you feel the time is right, conclude the meditation by opening your eyes.

When you go to sleep tonight and jump into bed, try giving this meditation again before you go to sleep. You will usually fall asleep and not remember the end of it, but your sleep will be more rejuvenating.

Once you learn this meditation for memory, it is also perfect for helping send you back to sleep if you often wake in the middle of the night and find it hard to get back to sleep.

Things to consider

Well done to those who did the reflective exercise and slayed the monkey mind! Awesome job!

If anyone couldn't break through, be patient and praise yourself for your efforts. With every confrontation you have, you'll become stronger and stronger, and once you beat it, every time you reface it from here you've already won. Your soul or spirit knows it.

Some people break through quite easily, whereas others find it more challenging. This part here is the greatest fear people have with meditating, and that is facing the monkey mind. I don't think they're scared, though, personally; I think it's their monitty.

If your job requires a lot of thinking, mental activity, or dealing with stress, incorporating a short meditation into your evening once you get home at night is the perfect tool to disconnect completely, enter the recesses of your heart, and leave what happened at work that day behind you.

This meditation on the shining white pearl of the heart holds an incredible alchemy to it. While you are practicing it, you are training yourself to center your thoughts and feelings, and because you bring your focus on nothing but the pearl, it becomes the point of letting go of the outer world around you and beginning the journey within.

Once you start fanning the fire of it with your breath, you are now starting to link the action of breathing to being at the nexus of your inner self. Which means after practicing this meditation, your breathing throughout the day in time, will be sustaining that connection to this. The last element of using the visual of the white light within the pearl as rejuvenating your body with your breath is incorporating a healing element into your meditation, which will also become an unconscious action in time while you breathe throughout the day.

In short, the more you practice this meditation and incorporate the breathing and visualizing this pearl or spiritual center, you'll begin breathing throughout your days in the same way as you would with your eyes closed in meditation.

4

Know Thyself: Unveiling Your True Identity

Now that we are beginning to make progress and build momentum with our meditations, we may experience moments throughout our days when we catch ourselves engaged in emotions or drifting off in thought.

Rather than being hard on ourselves, let us reflect on what is happening and ask ourselves soft and straightforward questions like:

- *"Why am I doing that?"*
- *"What is that feeling?"*
- *"What am I feeling this anxious for?"*

Or we can also start self-correcting by gently speaking softly in heart to ourselves with comments like:

- *"This thinking is unnecessary."*
- *"Stop thinking."*
- *"Stop this nonsense."*

Once we start to notice our thoughts and feelings drifting in the wrong direction, we have already begun to walk the path of mastering our thoughts and feelings for the better.

Before, there were a lot of unconscious things going on within us that we were ignorant of. The first step to fixing a problem for good is being able to see it surface.

Please be patient as we start this path of self correcting, as getting frustrated with ourselves will either make the task more difficult, make us feel uncomfortable, or lead us to give up.

And we don't want that at all.

With constancy, we will start to see a change in ourselves. You may even see feelings and clarity similar to those we have felt in our native state when meditating begin to surface while we actively function throughout our days.

This is the goal we want to hold in our hearts.

This is the goal we want to achieve.

This is the goal I'll be sharing every strategy that I can to help you close the door to your old ways for good and begin experiencing a life that is so much more fulfilling. Still, we must follow the process of reading the teachings in this book and applying them to our worlds if we want to enter these added dimensions I speak of.

Let us continue growing daily and aim to close those gaps quicker in steering ourselves to live a life of who we want to be, not the person we once were.

What are our four lower bodies?

If we take an esoteric approach and dissect or divide our psyche into four quadrants, similar to how you would cut a pie into four slices, the four slices or portions of ourselves would be labelled the physical, emotional, mental, and memory parts of ourselves.

This visual will help us better understand the requirements to bring ourselves into alignment and help us align a lot faster.

I will call the four quadrants of ourselves our four lower bodies, as it makes this part so much easier to understand. Also, once we begin aligning our four lower bodies, and they connect and come into balance, it becomes a platform for our soul or spirit to stand on. Let us visualize a four-sided pyramid and imagine each side of the pyramid's base, as each of our four lower bodies all evenly connected. With them all in balance and connected, our soul or spirit raises upwards to the point at the top of the pyramid, now sustained and supported by the four lower bodies beneath.

The pyramid's point then becomes the center of our conscious awareness as the four lower bodies merge and align.

This will give you a vision of what we aim for, but first, I'll explain the four lower bodies a little deeper.

The physical body

Your physical body is the densest of our four lower bodies. If you want, you can align it with the earth element. The physical body is the part of our being we can see, touch, and feel. Because our physical body is grounded and anchored in the physical plane, we need to eat correctly and have balanced sleeping patterns in order for it to function correctly.

Our physical body is our physical vehicle that we build and create with while serving all life around us. Out of the four lower bodies, this is the easiest of the four to master, provided we sleep and eat correctly and learn to stay disciplined and say no to ourselves in the face of temptation.

As we begin to become more mindful of the food we fuel our vehicle with, go to bed at a reasonable time to recharge ourselves and take time to be out in nature and sunshine, we develop a stronger intuition with our physical body to where we become more receptive to the signs it gives us, telling us what it needs to keep us balanced and functioning properly.

The emotional body

Our next body to focus on is our emotional body or feeling body. The emotional body is the part of our beings aligned with the water element. This is the part of us where we experience and govern our emotions and feelings. When you think of the ocean and how the waves increase and settle, it is similar to our feelings that rise and drop and give us contrast throughout the day. You can look at our emotions as being energy in emotion. Many people wrestle with this body the most out of the four, as it can push and pull us in different directions, leading us to feel inundated or lost at sea with our feelings. This is because this part of our being, in its proper form, is where our creative energies are governed the most while we 'build things' and create with our physical bodies.

Please note: When I refer to building things, this means making things in the physical plane, such as composing emails, cooking food, cleaning, writing, art, setting up a business, and any physical activity that can't be completed without our physical body. Our emotional body is supposed to motivate and drive the physical body to complete its tasks while mirroring the perfect energies of

42

life into our world.

Once we optimize our emotional body and this part of our body to emanate and creatively express positive emotions, this becomes a powerful driving force to help us with many things. Only through misuse of our creativity, governing the wrong energies and emotions into the world around us for long periods of time, do we experience negative and traumatic feelings.

We've cleared the desktop; now we have to reprogram the computer.

Being hard on yourself or hating yourself for the feelings arising will do nothing but make matters worse. Once we start acknowledging this part of our being, looking at it patiently for change, this part of ourselves will begin to listen and obey our desires and start correcting its patterns.

Remember, you are the captain of the ship. Don't be led to believe these four children are running the house!

The first step in correcting our emotional world is dealing with the years of suppressed emotions we've burrowed deep down in ourselves. We push it down and suppress it because dealing with the energy this way is easier than resolving and transmuting the feelings immediately. Then, in any event in our lives where we experience similar feelings, we tend to overreact as the older energy is trying to escape at the same time as the current energy you're dealing with.

This is often why people have the habit of becoming either really angry, really scared, really sexual, or really fanatical. Please don't judge anyone if you see any emotional patterns within them; this is merely to understand further how inordinate desires and negative emotions harbor within us and can become overwhelming.

We want to clear our emotions, go through the process of having everything surface, let go, reset, and bring this body to operate positively to help us in everything we do in the world. I will cover this process more deeply in the coming chapters.

The mental body

The mental body governs our mind and thoughts. Think of the wind element and in how the air travels, similar to how our mind operates and flows. The soft breeze can complement what it is we are looking at, but if it blows too strongly and loses control and balance, we find it hard to focus and can only see part of the picture.

The mental body is an excellent problem-solving tool and can help us greatly in life. Still, like the other two bodies, it's all about balance. If you overanalyze everything, thinking how smart you are, how smart are you really?

If the mental body is clean and clear, we become very visual. Often, if we are looking to create something, we can map it out in our minds and see it before we even begin building it. If we need an answer to a problem, we look to our mind, and if our mind is clear and we are heart-centered, the answer often descends into our vision, or the answer is given to us, followed by a feeling of certainty that this is the right thing to do. We visualize what we want to build, then the vision fuels our emotional body, which then gives us the desire to build it, then the desire to build it fuels our physical body to bring us into action and start building.

Ponder on this description of the mind fueling emotions, which then fuels the body to act and witness how this happens in everything we do.

The memory body

Lastly, the memory body contains our memories, playing a big part in programming the other three bodies to work for us on auto-pilot, like driving a car. This part of our being is aligned to the fire element. The memory body holds the memory of all the patterns of the three other bodies.

Whenever we see ourselves falling back into an old pattern that we are trying to change, quite often, it's because it's a habit we've accumulated over three or four decades. Going back to the example of driving the car, when we first started learning to drive, we were watching everything going on and consciously thinking about and making every action, to where now, we can jump in a car, drive, and arrive at our destination, but if we try and recall the drive itself, quite often it's hard to remember, as we were driving on auto-pilot. In other words, the memory body was driving.

This goes with every habit we have assigned to ourselves, good or bad. We have to consciously make the change and perform every action consciously to retrain ourselves and start completing the task automatically.

When we start to do this inner work in the laboratory of our beings, we pull apart those energy patterns that we don't want within ourselves anymore and replace the habit or action we are trying to remove with something else. It is essential to build a relationship with your memory body through the process and not beating yourself up or being hard on yourself, as it will make the whole reprogramming process much easier and faster.

The memory body has also been referred to as the etheric body, which refers to it as a vehicle for our soul or spirit to travel in once we start entering higher levels of consciousness within and build a stronger connection with our inner self.

At this stage, though, it's not necessary to go too deep into this purpose of the etheric body, as focusing on clearing the other three bodies will naturally help to clear this body, which will also help make those functions of this body clearer and more understandable in time, if that is what you are pursuing.

Saddle your four horses

That brief explanation of our four lower bodies is more so to prepare us for the following visualization. I want you to imagine a miniature version of yourself, standing about the size of your thumb and riding on a two-wheeled chariot. This smaller version of you if it helps, imagine it as being your soul or spirit.

Now, picture four horses pulling this chariot you are riding, and every horse riding in the same direction. These four horses are your four lower bodies. The second we see one of the horses steering off course, we have to pull the reins or crack the whip to bring that horse back on course to running with the other three.

For example:

· If one of your horses starts heading in the wrong direction, like your mind is wandering off in idle thought, crack the whip.

- Or your emotions start obsessing a little on something about to happen, crack the whip.
- If you see yourself snacking too much or overeating sugar in unhealthy amounts, crack the whip.

At this stage in our journey, focusing too much on one horse is not wise, but more so to see the four horses operating together in unity.

Reflective exercise: connection with our four lower bodies

After explaining the four quadrants of our psyche and the visualization of ourselves as the small version riding the chariot, I'd like you to take a second to reflect and visualize this again, eyes open or closed, whichever you prefer.

Now, see the miniature version of yourself within your heart on a chariot, holding the reins and controlling these four horses in front of you.

Softly squeeze your hands into gentle fists or touch your skin, linking that physical touch sensation with the horse on the far left in front of you. This horse is your physical body.

Next to that horse, see the horse, which is the emotional body. Breathe into your belly and feel the feeling in your solar plexus (the bottom of your rib cage), and link those feelings, good or bad, to being that horse in front of you, pulling the chariot forward.

The horse next to that one, see it now as your mental body. See your mind processing and thoughts linked to that horse before you. You can also breathe deeply through your nose to help you bring awareness to the area of your brain if needed. Once you become more aware of the location of your brain, link that location to the third horse in front of you, the mental body.

Lastly, see the fourth horse on our far right, the memory body, which holds the patterns and memories of the other three horses or bodies, enabling us to retain information to allow the other three to function and be programmed to operate habitually.

All four horses are equal, and all four horses are riding in unison.

After you see this, get up at your own pace. Go to the kitchen and pour yourself water or drink something. Try seeing the four horses saddled in front of you as you walk towards the place from where you are going to get this drink. Then, continue trying to hold onto this visualization of these imaginary horses in front of you as you pour the drink and sip on it, then keep focused on the visualization throughout the day for as long as possible.

Is your mind being quiet?

If not, crack the whip.

Meditation exercise: the white pearl aligns the four horses

In this meditation, we'll repeat the previous meditation but elaborate deeper and add more.

Let us get comfortable, sitting or lying down on our back, whatever you prefer, and begin by touching the center of your chest with your middle finger.

See the shining white pearl within the center of your chest.

Now close your eyes and draw your attention to it, breathing in the white light and fire coming from the pearl and then fan that fire as you breathe out.

Once you feel comfortable after several breaths, see your four horses riding in front of you.

- Imagine grabbing the reins and gently squeezing your hands together to help you rekindle your physical senses and the feeling of the physical horse.
- Now breathe into your stomach to tune into your feelings within your belly, and link those feelings to the feeling of your emotional horse.
- Then, breathe through your nose to sense your mind and the space in your mind, then connect to the space in your mind, linking it to the horse in front of you, which is your mental body.
- Lastly, see your memory body as the fourth horse before you riding next to the other three.

Holding the reigns, lead the horses so they enter into the light of the shining white pearl.

Let go of the reins and let them disappear into the pearl.

This shining white pearl intensifies in light and becomes brighter and brighter.

You see the pearl start expanding in size, then you walk towards it, entering the white fire of the pearl as well.

This shining white pearl is your doorway to higher levels of consciousness.

Feel the white pearl surrounding you like you are in a bubble's center.

You feel your whole body mirroring and become the same white firey light as the light around you.

Stay in this space for as long as possible.

When you are ready to return, open your eyes slowly, but try to hold your visualization as if standing within this white fire pearl for as long as possible.

Things to consider

Seeing the four quadrants of your being is the perfect way to balance all four quadrants of yourself. It seems more manageable when we dissect a task into pieces. Suppose you have one or two areas of yourself to bring back into balance. This is a perfect tool as you use the momentum of the other horses to get the horse or body pulled or whipped into alignment faster.

When this visual was given to me years ago, I found that I had no thoughts or feelings disturbing me so long as I visualized the four horses in front of me as I lived my day. You end up letting go of the reins in time, and by focusing purely on the shining white pearl, the pearl ends up holding onto your four horses.

After some time, your four lower bodies will become disciplined, so when you enter meditation, they enter that shining white pearl in the secret chamber of your heart that you have been focusing on.

From here, meditation becomes an even easier process to enter that state, for if you have feelings of discomfort, you know your emotional body still hasn't entered within. If your mind is still thinking, you'll know your mental body is still running around in the paddocks and needs to be saddled. If you drift off and start thinking about what happened in the day, you'll know your memory body has run off and needs to be whipped back in line. Or if you start feeling hungry, bored, or tense, you'll know your physical body hasn't entered within either. In time and with practice, you'll also be able to do this while you are conscious and active throughout your days in life.

If you start observing yourself throughout the day and look at your four lower bodies and how they function, both positively and negatively, you will start making major strides in self-mastery.

5

Your Native State: Returning to Inner Harmony

I trust now you're starting to see subtle changes within yourself in how you are experiencing things day to day.

Continue having your alarms going throughout the day to help you build the habit and skill of listening gracefully. This action of focusing only on listening to the sounds we hear around us, next to correctly breathing, is the most effective tool for realigning ourselves, as it pulls us away from our thoughts, gets us outside of our heads, and realigns us with the inner faculties of our being.

Through practice, like meditation, listening in this manner picks us up, realigns our being, and recharges us. Once we start seeing the benefit of emptying ourselves and listening to the sounds around us, we get excited. This means that while we do it, we feel joy because we now are listening with love. And this is where the magic begins.

Remember, we also have the first meditation exercise at our disposal. This simple practice of breathing in and out to the count of eight is a versatile tool that can be used whenever and wherever we need it. It's a quick and effective way to bring ourselves back to a state of feeling calm and focused, no matter the circumstances.

With the earlier exercises in the chapter on meditation, we should have faced ourselves, smashed through and caged the monkey mind several times now, at least.

We should be feeling more confident within ourselves.

Our four horses are now galloping together in more alignment. Things are starting to look more crystal clear. The feelings we hold of being more connected and closer to our inner self is serene.

You've managed to still my mind, now what?

Do it again. Rome wasn't built in a day. Look at this challenge of changing these elements of yourself with nothing but joy, as now we know what we need to work on, so let's get to work. You will quickly see massive changes within yourself by following everything this book has instructed.

Understand, though, that we are plucking out habits within ourselves that have often gone on unknowingly for twenty or thirty years, maybe even more. By focusing on building these new habits, they start to become subconscious, and in time, they become unconscious, and we begin performing them automatically. This is what we want.

Can you see a little more about our fourth horse's purpose, the memory body, and how it comes into play in helping us lead the other three?

Suppose we can dedicate the next couple of weeks to start living our lives, incorporating these simple meditations I have shared, and practicing to function with our thoughts and feelings in check. In that case, we will start forging a new identity for ourselves. Life for us will start changing in every way and for the better.

Heart-centered versus head-centered

One of the greatest fallacies I've ever heard is that the brain is in the center of our universe and the most important organ in our body. Look at all the Egyptian hieroglyphs, Leonardo Divinci's depiction of man, and the ancient civilizations' illustrations; most of the drawings on the walls of men and women have been drawn with the heart highlighted on the image. They saw that the heart is the center of our universe, not the mind. It has only been in the last two hundred years that the concept that the brain is running the show has really crept in.

The mind is the most incredible tool when it is serving the heart. Take a second to do a search online for yourselves. Search for the term 'heart intelligence' and see what comes up. Many scientific studies and institutes support what I am saying.

As we have been working on aligning our four lower bodies and leading them to enter the shining white pearl within the center of our being, we can see we have already started the journey to becoming more heart-centered.

Are you starting to see the alchemy within this book and how everything is starting to fall into place?

If you are, I promise you, it's about to get a lot more awesome in the upcoming chapters ahead. When we look to our hearts for answers, the greatest wisdom and wisest answers come to us with ease. When we speak from the heart, people connect with us and trust what we have to say, as they can feel our words.

Our ultimate goal is to see a miniature version of ourselves standing or sitting within our hearts, governing the ship, or riding the chariot.

The easiest way to achieve this is by continuing to be more mindful in every moment, breathing while visualizing our inner self, and bringing the thoughts and emotions back into the center of our chest, and into our heart.

Another level of mastery

By practicing to become more heart-centered, we start entering another level of mastery.

You may notice that after living at the level of our hearts or within our hearts for some time, there may be moments when someone says something out of line to us. Our response won't come from the ego, which is at the level of the belly. That's because our focus on being heart-centered has brought us above the belly.

When we act or react from the level of the heart, our words are warmer, our points raised often hold more sense, and the other person is more likely to hear us. Next time someone starts arguing with you, if you mirror their energy with your response, they'll hit the ball back to keep the rally going, no matter what point you try to make.

In contrast, if you let their energy pass you and don't attach yourself to it, take a breath or smile before you respond, keeping your words coming from the level of your heart, it doesn't mean you've lost the match; the score is fifteen, love.

Love in harmony; the harmony in love. Life becomes much easier as we start swimming with the waves of life and not against them. When we are heart-centered, our four horses are in alignment, and the foundation is laid for our inner self to lead us even more. You will find you may enter shops, or be walking through the day and feel almost a forcefield around yourself. That's because you have entered into your heart and are starting to function in everyday life while in this space.

This is a good thing!

This means have made massive strides upwards on this path that we are walking.

You have one foot in each world now.

The outer and the inner.

You know how to survive in the outer world; I mean, you've done it all your life. You can turn away from this path anytime you want and return to playing in the garden with everyone else instead of entering the castle, for you are a creature of free will.

Let us explore this inner world a little more, as there is still so much magic to share.

Listen for the prompting

With our four lower bodies a little clearer and our minds not clouded by thought, you can imagine four clear planes of glass stacked on top of one another. You could see through them if you were holding the sheets of glass before you.

Our thoughts and feelings aren't as clouded, which pulls apart the curtains, allowing rays of light to shine through and light the room of our being.

Just as we have been meditating and picking the internal point within ourselves of the shining white pearl to hold our focus on, we can now use that point of focus as a doorway to something more.

Let us start by asking for more guidance from our inner intuition, asking our hearts a question, and then waiting patiently for the answer.

Practice it.

Whether we close our eyes and go within, or if we whisper the question quietly to ourselves, we can ask that point within anything at all that's going on in our day-to-day lives: whether it is what we need to do or the choice we should make with something, just ask a question and wait patiently.

Occasionally, our mind can trick us into pretending it's that guidance, giving us an answer through thought.

Cheeky little monkey!

What we are listening for is that soft, still voice within our hearts.

It almost sounds like an angel.

Maybe it is?

Who knows at this stage?

Through my experience, I have found that everything it has said to me is always right. Even if it wasn't the answer I wanted to hear at the time. It has never given me the wrong advice when I have obeyed its guidance and followed it. Looking back and reflecting on all the times I have not willingly listened to it, I see now that I was wrong.

The hardest thing is that once we become aware of it, we catch ourselves consciously going against its guidance and choosing to do what we want to do because it seems like that is best for us now. I assure you, it's not.

Say this out aloud,

"We will grow from a no, but not from a yes."

Remember that line the next time your lesser or lower self is

57

trying to run the show.

Anytime I go against the guidance of my inner self, I always surrender and admit I was wrong for not following its direction. There is no point in being stubborn and building a wall to block it out; time is too short for that. Once you start following this inner prompting, put your full trust in it. Life improves and changes quickly, so get ready for it.

I want to bring your attention to Mahatma Gandhi on this topic, for one of his quotes really stuck out to me, which may also for you,

"The only tyrant I accept in this world is the 'still small voice' within me."

Look up his achievements if you can and see all that this man achieved in his life. He stopped civil wars and brought so many people together; if this man's inner guidance has helped him to leave a footprint in human history, imagine what it could do for you?

This is a personal journey. This voice will be your trusted guide through life, even in the darkest times, if you surrender everything and trust in it. The first thing, though, is to speak to it. Ask it questions. Wait for answers, and if you are blessed enough to hear its guidance, trust in what it is saying is right and obey it. You will not regret it.

Reflective exercise: the biggest problem you are facing?

What is one thing that is weighing on your shoulders right now?

If you could change this problem, would it make you feel much lighter?

I want you to take some time to speak about it in your heart.

Choose your favorite meditation in the book so far to really slow yourself down for a minute or two, then start speaking to your heart as if you were venting out to a close friend or family member.

It can feel a little stupid to start with; like you're talking to yourself.

Have the courage to keep discussing the problem that is burdening you and how it is limiting your progress.

Speak about what you want to achieve.

Share what you believe has stopped happening in your life and how easier life would be for you if you really overcame it.

Then, ask your heart what you must do to resolve it, and wait silently for the answer.

If the answer doesn't come to you right away, be patient. If you can't hear the prompting or answer, love this initiation of patience that you are being initiated on with your whole heart and know what you want, then let it go.

The call compels the answer.

If you haven't heard an answer yet, surrender, and let go. Even if you don't get a direct answer given to you now directly, once you start to focus on the issue again in future, the answer will trickle down somehow to you through events around you if you are searching for it.

For what you desire, that you'll manifest.

I've said this several times to you now. Are you starting to get it?

Meditation exercise: your tropical island

Before you begin this meditation, I want you to jump online and search for the term 'tropical island beach' to give you an image of what you'll be visualizing in front of your mind. After you do that, I want you to sit comfortably or lie down. Close your eyes and begin the process of our earlier meditations.

You see that shining white pearl within the secret chamber of your heart, drawing your attention and breathing from and into the pearl.

Now, let your four lower bodies enter into the shining white pearl and walk through after them into the dazzling white transcendent light, seeing yourself standing barefoot on this perfect tropical island.

- Feel your feet sinking into and absorbing the warmth of the sand beneath you.
- See the crystal clear aquamarine water sparkling in the sunlight and blending with the perfect blue sky.
- With not one cloud in sight, the blue sky stretches as far as you can see.
- The calming waves gently soothe your heart as each wave breaks onto the sand on the shore of the beach.
- You sit down and absorb the perfection around you in this perfect place.
- You can smell the salt water as you breathe in deeply through your nose.
- Each breath you take is invigorating.
- You feel a warm and gentle inviting breeze from one side of you.
- The sound of birds occasionally can be heard in the background.

Love fills your heart in reaction to every one of your senses being stimulated by this perfect scene.

This is your place.

This is your tropical island.

This is a special place you can go to whenever you want from now on.

Enjoy your time in solitude for as long as you need.

Things to consider

With the reflective exercise in this chapter, if it doesn't resonate with you at this stage, let it go. I have written this book with the intent that my readers will revisit this book, re-reading it more than once.

There are deeper layers within these words to help you take every step that is needed to connect with your inner self, which is the ultimate goal in hindsight.

Still, if this is unimportant to you right now, that's completely okay. Keep following the book; as much as you can, and by the end, you will have many tools in your arsenal and keys to take away to start bringing into your world.

With the meditation of your perfect tropical island beach, if you prefer the view of a rocky waterfall, a mountain peak, a forest, a crystal cave, or a spiritual altar, then I encourage you to find an image online of that place to help you visualize it through the meditation and go through the exercise again and spend some time there providing you follow the steps and travel there through centering and entering your heart, and walking into the shining white pearl.

The secrets within this book are contained within this shining white pearl and will make the following chapters easier for you if you experiment with seeing it in your meditations now.

Not to mention, by following these steps and entering the shining white pearl to travel to this special place, when you return and open your eyes, you will feel invigorated, calm, and balanced.

Hey, who's to say you can't have two or three different places you can go to when you meditate?

Or maybe even more...

6

Embrace Your Inner Child: Rediscovering Joy and Innocence

And now the fun begins. Keep reconnecting with the center of your being whenever you feel out of sorts, and continue practicing the meditations I have shared with you: after work, before dinner, and before you retire at night.

Try to keep cultivating the art of listening gracefully with every conversation from now on, and that is listening with no opinion on what you want to say next, with your thoughts and mind completely still.

You can also start focusing on your heart as if you had a third ear within it, listening to every sound around you or when people speak to you.

That shining white pearl I have been speaking of through the meditations is the point you should be listening from. By doing this, we focus on that point within our being that brings us into contact with higher planes of consciousness.

With that all in mind, let's step things up.

If you can, I want you to remember a moment in your childhood, playing in the backyard, completely captivated and lost in the moment. Now look at the world through the eyes of that younger version of yourself, playing and having so much fun.

We had a joy for life back when we were this age, living purely from moment to moment.

This is how we were designed to be. Still, through years of schooling and over-educating our analytical minds with curriculum, we became conditioned to believe that every moment we experienced had to be analytically processed and categorized.

Poppycock!

Make a decision with me to drop this nonsense and watch how quickly and smarter you become in how you function.

Yes, it's true; the mind can give us an answer to everything around us.

But here is the problem...

It makes everything you experience in life about you: your opinion on things, your analysis of things, your commentary on things, your calculations on things; the world is nothing but your perspective. Then, your perspective of the world revolves around nothing but your ego and sense of self.

Life isn't just about you.

This isn't about you at all.

This has nothing to do with you.

Yes, you are the one experiencing everything around you, but the part of you doing all the self-talk on your experiences isn't...

Ah huh! Busted!

Can you see that?

Got ya!

This part of you is so sneaky and most cunning. When you

catch it, it escapes your view, retreating and swimming deeper into the waters until out of sight, and will not surface again until when you least expect it.

This is a constant battle we will face daily until we align our four lower bodies and rise higher.

Nonetheless, the first step to overcoming this is listening gracefully, as you're rebuilding your processing to listen and just observe, which silences the ego and monkey mind. As you become more comfortable with listening in this manner, empty from all opinions and sense of self, content, and in a 'graceful silence', you'll start seeing life through a new lens. Life becomes fun just by watching and listening to what's happening around you. You don't need to try to create a moment through speaking, for the moments already there.

You then begin to hear conversations around you and hang on to every word when people around you speak. It's like you feel a child at heart again, but there is still more to unfold after this.

Your inner child

Whether you have children or not is irrelevant. Next time you sit down, rest your hands on your lap with your hands open and your palms facing up.

Does it feel comfortable?

Imagine you're holding a little child. Beautiful and perfect, and unconditioned by all the analytic fanatics of this world we live in.

Now comfort them as if you were a parent settling a young, scared child.

This child is you.

This child is the perfect version of yourself; I know you can feel it.

However, we often lose touch with this part of ourselves when that tyrant ego enters our psyche. That bossy, demanding child controlling their surroundings to get what they want, pushing our inner child out of the limelight.

This sounds extreme, but i must illustrate it like this to help better discern the two different temperaments of ourselves.

I am bringing this up so you can identify these different layers of self. It is not for you to dwell on the past or what has happened.

This inner child is a part of you. If you choose to focus on familiarising yourself with them more, you will go through the most remarkable healing and resolution within yourself.

You will feel more fulfilled and whole as a person.

Please note: I'm not a trained psychologist. I am explaining this to give you a general overview, raise your awareness of the different layers of the psyche, and help you overcome these lower levels and step up higher.

I have composed this book to help you on your quest for self-mastery and to identify different levels and areas of ourselves that we were previously unaware of.

More importantly, our inner child is the genuine part of us we need to reconnect with before our soul or spirit can rise up within that point in our hearts to the level of our inner self.

If you would like to further pursue building this connection to your inner child, I suggest you start with the book "The Inner Child Workbook" by Cathryn L. Taylor.

In saying that, let us continue.

By practicing graceful silence throughout your day and taking even just a minute to rest your hands on your lap and connect with that inner child daily, you'll familiarize yourself with a part of you that needs nurturing to help you grow in wholeness.

From there, if you wish to take this further, you can consider taking time out once a week at least to help you connect even more with your inner child. Even if it is for half an hour, take some time to do something creative like: drawing, cooking, coloring in a coloring-in book, or anything you loved to do when you were younger.

If you are coloring in a coloring book, for example: imagine you're either coloring in the coloring book with your inner child next to you watching or coloring-in with you, or even better, imagine your inner child is within you and is the one coloring-in the coloring book.

You can also take moments in solitude or out in nature where you acknowledge that your inner child is walking or standing with you.

Depending on how deep you are going on this journey, you can use your inner child as the platform for your new refined self. By focusing on your inner child, you also focus on your soul or spirit, as both are connected.

No matter what you have done in your life that you are not proud of, that was yesterday and means nothing now. Finding and raising your inner child is how you make things right, rebuild yourself, and become that perfect person you know with all your heart you want to be.

Just remember, you are already perfect if you focus on your inner child within you and start raising them correctly.

How to beat the tyrant ego

If you have thoughts or feelings about beating yourself up about the past, that isn't you; that's the tyrant ego. It has no place within you anymore now you've found your inner child, so of course, it's going to try and draw your focus on it so you're looking at it and not your inner child.

Let it try and point the finger at everyone else, tearing down its surroundings.

This thing is nowhere.

Now we understand this more, why would anyone choose to engage with this over their inner child?

If you find the thoughts or self-talk consistent and intrusive, don't react or respond to them and get pulled into the argument. This will do nothing but wear you down and burn you out. Just respond with love and focus on your heart. By putting your focus on your heart, it can't steal your energy anymore and will eventually fade away and cease to exist.

If this doesn't work, remember you also have a castle now. Enter the secret chamber within your heart and close the door. It won't be able to touch or disturb you, as it's not allowed to enter.

Everything walks away when you are in this room or castle because it knows you've won the battle.

This battle with the tyrant ego was tough for me, as I was unaware I had a castle to enter and protect me, making it a war that went on for years. It won't be for you, because you have a castle.

And who is the king of the castle?

Your inner self.

Now you can protect your inner child and keep them safe

within the walls of this castle. They've probably been bullied by this tyrant ego for years, regardless of whether you consciously ever heard any of the name-calling and trauma they've been put through on lower levels by the tyrant-ego and other things.

There is no reason for your inner child to leave the castle walls from now on.

Look after them and love them and find your wholeness.

Have you ever thought about why life changes for someone when they become a parent?

Some people say it feels like they are reborn again?

It's because the adult gets a glimpse again of how to see the world through the eyes of a child, which takes them back to relive those memories of the wonderful years they had themselves growing up, which brings them to reconnect with their inner child and begin those years again in growing up.

Spend more time with children

To anyone who is a parent, this part is so important!

Nonetheless, if you have siblings or friends with children, you should also listen closely to this part .

So many people in this world talk 'at' children and not 'to' them, treating their time with them like every other interaction they have in their day-to-day lives.

Then you see that analytical intellect creeping in, persuading you that you are above them and how they know very little about life.

Nonsense!

Rather than effortlessly talking to them the next time you are in a child's company, let these words stick and prompt you...

Stop, re-centre yourself, and ask them what they are doing or did today.

Then, let them lead the conversation.

Listen to them speak in the way that I have been asking you repeatedly to listen, and that is empty of thought and with zero ego.

If you are only listening to them, watch them lead you into their world in terms of how they view their lives and what they are experiencing.

What many are unaware of is that if you are speaking with a child at the age of five, you go back to those years of your life when you were five years old, enabling you to access that part of your inner child's development, and you start re-living it with the child as you interact with them. This gives you an added opportunity to find wholeness within yourself while you spend time with them. The same would go for if you are interacting with an eight-year-old, a thirteen-year-old, or a child of any age, and that is, you return to those years of the age of the child you are spending time with.

It makes the so-called burden of becoming a parent actually one of the greatest opportunities for finding wholeness.

I have three daughters, and while raising the first two, I was unaware that all of this was happening, but I am sure it still was to a certain extent.

I learned about this before my youngest daughter was born, which has made every day of raising her so incredible as I am aware of it. She is almost five now, which excites me for the years to come. I also have it with the other two now, which is incredible to watch us all grow together. If you are a parent and have children, keep this in mind and try this for yourself. Even if you can't see it immediately, watch how much more the children will start to love and respect you and lovingly obey your words when you become a child with them, rather than being that boring, unfair bad guy or girl always telling them off and not letting them have any fun.

Now, to add another layer of awesomeness to this, when you are playing with children and having fun, picture that your inner child is also playing with them. This means you are being an awesome parent or person while also finding wholeness at the same time.

Set your alarm to re-connect five times a day

Take a moment to set your phone to have an alarm reminder five times a day from now on.

Let's step things up a little.

Every phone nowadays has this feature, so there are no excuses.

Not with a loud alarm; just set it to vibrate on silent. So, if it's in your pocket, you are prompted and reminded what to do.

Once you receive the prompting from your alarm, focus on the shining white pearl within your heart and breathe in deeply through your nose, seeing the air breathing into the pearl within your heart, then hold your breath in. You can also imagine the air you are holding in as being love, if that helps; after a second or two, breathe out through your mouth.

- *Pause from reading for a second and try this now for one or two breaths.*

You may do the eight counts for each breath and in between,

similar to the earlier meditation; that is up to you. As we breathe, though, our primary focus is on re-connecting to our spiritual center.

After several breaths, once you feel a little more centered, try imagining breathing the energy of the white fire within that shining white pearl as you breathe in, and as you breathe out, see that white fire in your breath now spreading all through your body and filling every cell of your being.

Try to focus on moving the white fire through your body while you breathe throughout the day today for as long as you can. If you do, this will build a solid foundation for building a habit that will last forever.

Count to three

Now, we are more centered within ourselves; the only thing stopping us from staying centered is the outer distractions of others. The first thing we can do to keep on top of this is control how we interact and react with people in our daily lives.

When spoken to or asked a question, try counting to three in your heart before you respond. Let your response come from that shining white pearl within your heart, and then witness how your days will start transforming.

Adding this calculated pause before you react to others will change your life in many ways.

When people speak, they unknowingly dump their stress and emotions on others. Not to mention, everyone has that mon-ster swimming around in their unconscious that occasionally surfaces, overreacts, and roars at everyone, leading us to say all those horrible things we often regret later on once we have calmed down again.

If our response comes from the heights of our hearts, we block the door that thing sneaks through to snap and roar at others, as it can't exist where there is love.

Trust me with this: try to start reflecting from now on every time you lose your cool and say something you regret. Observe if you were speaking at the level of your heart when it happened or from the level of your belly.

Practice speaking less

So many people today depend on feel-good idle chatter for a temporary high to pick them up throughout the day. We no longer need that high, for we've found how to lift our energies and cultivate happiness.

I am not saying you should not speak with friends and loved ones and continue having those deep conversations with connection.

You may even share with them this incredible new book you are reading and tell them about all the awesome things you are learning from it and how it's helping you.

That's one thing I am actually encouraging ;)

Do you see what I did there?!?

What I am referring to are those day-to-day transactions and conversations at work, etc.

Everything is about balance and finding what works for you.

It takes a lot of effort to take on this new approach of being heart-centered with all your verbal communication and to rebuild habits within yourself so that every response comes from your heart, not your ego.

It's worth it! If you can do this, you will start rising faster to new heights of understanding life.

Catch yourself out

The more we start living life centered within our hearts, the more we'll start to see our worlds cut in two in a sense. There will be moments where we'll feel all switched on and in alignment, feeling good about ourselves, then suddenly find ourselves drawn into some conversation with someone or caught up in some moment that distracts us, and we fall back into our old selves again.

This is completely okay. This is actually a sign that we are starting to make permanent changes within; we just need to find the quickest and easiest way to close that gap quicker from the time we spend falling back into our old selves and switch back to spending more time forging this new identity we are beginning to build.

Are you starting to see why the daily alarms are so important now?

We can go on for hours operating in life, completely forgetting about our goals, and that's because, sadly, most people on the planet are operating at that level of the ego. Often, it's easier to drop down to that level and follow them than to lift the world around us to the level of our hearts.

If you have made it this far on the path of self-discovery, where you start to identify and catch yourself when you're duped down in the matrix, then try to have a little fun with it.

Have fun catching yourself out next time you see that you've dropped to that level of everything else around you.

You can playfully say to yourself,

"Ah ha! Got ya!"

Remember, with all the practice you have been giving on re-centering yourself with your breath, you should only be one or two breaths away from re-centering yourself, re-entering into that focus on the shining white pearl, and connecting within.

If you want this new version of you, be patient; the changes are already starting to happen. Self-mastery is the key from here.

Be careful with your phone

We have to become more mindful of our phones. The year that I am writing this is the start of 2024, and already I get email notifications, SMS alerts, phone calls, and apps hooking me into having a look at them, and if I open up Facebook, then it's on! Game over! I am pulled into the matrix.

If you have to respond to work-related matters, focus on that connection with your heart and hold it before you pull it out of your pocket and view it.

Sometimes, there may be something urgent you have to respond to; if not, try ignoring it. You'd be surprised at the amount of things dumped on us first but then resolved by others if we don't take them on instantly.

It's essential to see that by rescuing others all the time and fighting their battles for them, we often find ourselves taking away the opportunity they have to grow by overcoming it themselves.

Again, this is general advice you must discern for yourself when taking on a problem. I am directing this more to readers who have a habit of rescuing others or super-productive people, where often work tasks are dumped on you because you are a doer and find it hard to say no to things. It's funny; I've seen many workplaces where eighty percent of the workload is done by ten to fifteen percent of the staff.

Learn to be able to surrender easily

Not many people know the true meaning of surrender and its importance for you, not just once, but daily.

Surrendering is letting go of something for a greater love. For some, it is harder to let go than for others, but once you learn to let go, it is a liberating gift that will instantly erase any sense of struggle.

Have you ever been spring cleaning your house and throwing away a lot of your old unused possessions and come across something that you were attached to, where you felt that sense of wanting to hold onto it, but you pursued throwing it out anyway, and overcame that sense of attachment?

That is surrendering. I know this example doesn't seem to have much to do with the topic in discussion. Still, it is a commonly experienced test, and I am sure everyone has experienced it at least once.

When we want something to happen or are holding onto something, that attachment of human will or stubbornness is what we need to break through, and the only way to do that is by surrendering.

Once you understand the truth in this, you see the magic involved with surrendering. Anytime you find yourself in a pickle or being tested on something, I have two words for you...

Remember surrender

Here we go. Let me give you some examples:

You're arguing with a loved one, work colleague or friend. Things are firing up to the point where the argument isn't

about the argument anymore but more about winning and hurting the other person

The winner of the argument is the first one to surrender. Surrendering is not submitting; that is different again. Surrendering is letting go of wanting to win the battle and hurting the other person. You are now becoming the bigger person in the situation and aligning your creative energies to start putting out the fire you've started rather than throwing more fuel on it.

There is a problem you're wrestling with, or you're having the worst day where everything going wrong for you

This can become difficult when you are trying to break through those blocks to your day or when it seems like all you've been doing all day is putting out fires.

You have been pushing yourself to break through and overcome the problem. It feels like you're either carrying the world on your shoulders or you are getting pushed and pulled in different directions, making it a struggle to deal with.

You need to pause for a second, stand still, breathe in through your nose, re-align, and stand tall and affirm to yourself to surrender.

Once you let go, that struggle vanishes. If you still are feeling the desire to fix the issue or stay busy, stop.

That's not you.

Are you starting to see that other part of yourself more now?

Look at the problem or issue and smile, knowing you will solve it. Once you re-align your feelings to love as you look at the issue at hand, then get to work.

You have so many things going on right now, and you're over your head

All of us have a problem with taking on too much, so much so it can often burn us out at times. If you ever find yourself caught with too big of a workload, you may need to drop something. Look at your workload and all the tasks. Have you taken on something recently that you can drop for now?

Is there something you can push out till tomorrow?

Are you operating with all these things on paper, or are you trying to juggle them all in your head?

Haven't you been listening to a word I've said?!?

If this is the case, do the same thing, stop, then surrender. Take a short, deep breath and re-center. Then, write out what needs to be done on a list and pick one task to do at a time, and then finish it, mark it off and move on to the next one.

Someone close to you are struggling but wont take your advice

This is a tough one, especially for parents and siblings. We are all on this planet learning lessons in life, some at different speeds than others. As much as it hurts to watch them go through the process, this needs to be done in order for them to grow.

Maybe there is pride or rebellion within them, wanting to prove you wrong?

People often carry this around with them.

Let's hope they succeed.

If not, mind your own business unless they ask you for help. Let's focus on ourselves and look at the test we are facing right now.

It is an inordinate desire to control others, so let it go.

Remember surrender...

Take a second to reset yourself and smile at what's going on, stand back and, as hard as it is, wait for them to reach out to you. Don't say another word about it until they do.

They will love and respect you so much for giving them space to learn this lesson for themselves.

There are many more tests we face daily where we often need to surrender; these are just a couple of examples that may show up in the days ahead for you to ponder on.

Surrender the outer world and step up higher

You may be reaching a level to where you feel you want to accelerate and step up higher. If this is the case, let us start looking around us and consider if there may be more levels to this physical plane than we are currently aware of.

Etheric and physical, form and formless, spirit and matter, it doesn't matter what language you use to try and explain it; let us just try focusing on finding it.

Whether you are sitting, standing, inside, outside, for any-thing to exist within the physical plane, it has to also exist in the formless or etheric plane as well, meaning that, as we look at the trees around us, the furniture in our house, every single object around us within our vision co-exists on a higher plane as well.

You have already witnessed this. Allow me to prove it.

Anytime you may have meditated for some time, opened your eyes and returned to, you may have witnessed, that you are more connected and feel at one with everything around you. It's like the world around you is different from when you first closed your eyes.

That is because when you close your eyes and still your mind, your consciousness expands, opening you to the formless, or etheric plane of where you are in meditation. Because your eyes are closed to the physical, you operate internally in this other realm or plane just above the physical.

Ponder on this next time you meditate.

If this is the case, and we know how good we feel when returning from meditating, why don't we start looking to try and have that connection in life all the time?

It is possible, believe me.

Let us start by bringing our attention to it in moments throughout the day.

If you are at your computer work desk: the desk, the computer, your pens, and the calculator, look at them and see the formless version in the higher etheric plane, either within or on top of the physical version you are looking at. Now pick the object up, hold it in your hands, and surrender the physical object your holding into the etheric version or formless version, and let go of the concept you are holding something just physical.

Now draw your attention towards yourself, knowing that for your physical self to exist, there has to be an etheric version of you as well. Draw your attention to it. You may wish to close your eyes and explore this further or continue operating in your day, but see everything around you as both physical with an identical version on top of it.

The floor your walking on...

The people you speak to...

Once your soul or spirit rises up into this etheric plane and to the level of your inner self, everything I am explaining will make so much more sense.

Are you still with me?

Or did I lose you for a second?

Or maybe you may have experienced something reading these words but want to understand them better. If that's the case, may I suggest that with your five daily alarms, after you re-connect and align yourself, you take not even a minute to focus on this etheric plane of formlessness above the physical around you? Even after one day of adding this to your five alarms, you'll see massive shifts within yourself and that plane will become more real.

The more you draw your attention to this etheric plane while looking at everything around you, the more you'll find yourself entering into it.

Start tuning into love

I want you to visualize an old radio with manual dials where you must turn the dial to tune into the channels and adjust the volume.

As you see the dial in your mind, imagine that dial as being able to control your emotions, and you can tune into channels of different emotions by twisting the dial.

Our emotions are a part of our creative energies that become a driving force in all we do; this is why we need to use them and have them operating in our favor.

- So play around for a second, and imagine you're tuning into the feeling of anger.
- Now, try tuning into the feeling of fear.

- Not interested in that one anymore, what about if we tune into the feeling of joy?
- Awesome... I like that. Now let's try love...

This is my favorite station, and I liked being tuned into bringing it into my world.

I trust this will also become your favorite station too.

Love can be the driving force behind everything we do.

This exercise of tuning the dial of your feelings to where you can adjust them will make it much easier to get out of a rut of emotion if you build a habit with it.

When we feel anger, fear, or anything inharmonious surface within us, we can simply pretend and imagine we are turning a dial in front of us and tune back into the radio station we want to feel... Love.

This may sound a little far-fetched at first, but if you play around with it for a bit, you might find you are able to pull yourself away from feeling negative feelings with ease and re-direct them to feel better, more positive feelings. You are the one who creates the energy you are feeling, after all, and you can't blame anyone else around you for what you are feeling.

What do you have to lose by trying this?

Listen and remember these words as if they were written in gold as I say them. The greatest gift in life is love. It is the greatest jewel that we can hold in our hands. It is the greatest gift we can share with others, create with, build with, act with, and greet any problem we face.

We all know in our hearts that this is true.

This is the force to life.

This is the language that everyone recognizes on a soul and spirit level, and the more you give with this love, the more rewarding it becomes as more love comes back to us. It keeps snowballing and builds to become more intense, to where the curtains to life open to help us see life's true purpose.

The whole world is looking for love.

Will you work on this area of your life and give the world what they are looking for?

I am overwhelmed with so much gratitude right now for being able to share this key to life with you.

It has changed my life for the better, and life for me just keeps getting better, and better, by the day.

But this is not about me.

This is about you.

I hope my testimony to this truth has transferred something onto you.

Let us explore together how to cultivate more love in our world.

Reflection exercise: what do you love doing?

I want you to grab your pen and paper now and spend a second brainstorming and mindmapping everything you love doing: fixing the car, cooking your favorite meal, watching your favorite series, doing your morning fitness, doing gardening on Saturdays, playing the piano, listening to music, dancing, drawing on paper, being intimate with a loved one, or drinking a beer out in the sun.

Whatever it is, write your list down on paper.

Try to get at least four or five things written down. Then, please look at each activity and start thinking about it and how you feel while you're doing the activity.

- *Can you feel any positive feelings within yourself?*
- *Can you feel anymore connected to your heart?*

If any feelings surface, this is just because as you recall those experiences, your body reacts, bringing up and starting to express the positive feelings you have linked to doing that activity. These are all your memories of the good times while performing that action.

Now, let's hold onto those feelings we are feeling and experiment a little. Spend at least thirty seconds experimenting with each question:

- *Can you increase the feeling at all by focusing on it?*
- *Can you see an imaginary dial in front of you and turn it up to increase the intensity of the feeling?*
- *Feeling this feeling of love, can you focus on it while you are breathing?*
- *Can you see this love everywhere around you and breathe it in and out, putting the feeling of love behind your breath?*

Close your eyes now for a second. Focus on your breathing and the love linked to those activities.

See if you can connect and intertwine the two.

Send as much time as you need to experiment with this.

Once you open your eyes, you may journal your thoughts and experiences. Remember, if you write out your experience on paper, it will cement it into your subconscious.

Meditation exercise: your secret star

For this meditation, we can close our eyes, centering all of our thoughts and energies into the center of our hearts.

Once you feel your mind and thoughts settle and saddle to the rhythm of your breath, imagine a star shining brightly above you.

It is about twenty feet above you.

You send it love and notice it starts sending love back to you simultaneously.

It feels identical to your heart, only bigger.

With all your energies and attention focused on it, you feel a thread of contact between your heart and this star of love above you.

Let everything other than this star above you fade away to nothing, focusing on nothing other than your breathing and the feeling of love from this star.

Feel that love from this star above filling your heart as it starts to intensify more and more.

Send all the love of your heart back into this star at the greatest intensity you can reach and hold it at that level of intensity.

Don't try to force or push the feeling of love. Imagine your body being nothing more than an empty cup, then seeing the love and light of this star filling your body until you completely mirror its radiance.

As above, so below.

You feel yourself entering into that shining white pearl within your heart and leaving your body, travelling up this chord into the center of the star above you.

Life, as you know it, stops.

You begin to enter a new level of awareness.

You feel you can see the whole world through the eyes of

this star and even further. The radiance shines needle like rays through all parts of your being, sending love in every direction.

At this level of consciousness, spend some time in silence within the heart of this star, sending love and light through its needle like rays in all directions, connecting you to everything on the planet and even further.

When you feel it is time to return, descend down the chord and re-enter into your heart.

You still feel the star above you shining, love. The love in your heart now shines simultaneously with the heart of the star above.

When you feel like concluding the meditation, open your eyes and thank your heart and this secret star above you for the experience that has been given to you.

Do not share your experience with anyone.

This is between you and your secret star.

From this point on, you can choose this star above you to be an extension of your heart, allowing you to bless life and those around you even more.

Things to consider

This exercise of jotting down the hobbies or activities we love doing is an exercise to help us find more love in our hearts. When we think of them, our memories of the experience can raise the feeling of love through all the love we have anchored into that activity. If it doesn't work or you find it confusing, don't get caught up or waste more energy on it; move forward and keep reading.

By the time you finish reading this book, you will better understand yourself. The more time you spend in meditation, the more these positive feelings will become dominant in your emotional expression, and you will be able to express them more freely.

The meditation on our secret star is incredible and one that I have been practicing for years.

I challenge you to give this meditation ten minutes daily, every day, for a week and watch your life change for the better.

Life changes, as you are not just heart-centered; it's like you are connected and vibrating with something higher. This meditation is probably one of the most powerful exercises I have included in this book. If you are consistent with it, that connection to that star above you never leaves you. It stays with you even when you open your eyes.

Then, when you start sending love into the world, you simultaneously feel the love being sent from above you. It is truly magical and one you need to experience for yourself to truly understand.

7

The Essence of Love: Understanding Its True Power

Love is limitless...

Understanding love is our key to the kingdom in living life.

Suddenly, every moment becomes a moment where we can react or express more love. The rewards are incredible, for what we send out into the world comes back tenfold like a boomerang, and life starts to become this divine romance to where we are in a constant state of happiness, feeling uplifted with every moment being transpired around us.

To those hearing my words and not feeling what I am sharing, I want you to be patient, for I will transfer some tips and tricks on how to tune into this feeling of love even more through this chapter.

We have virtually the whole planet slaving away, working their entire lives, holding the faith, that this will bring them that ideal partner and it is only through having a partner that we can feel complete and experience a life filled with love.

Bollocks!

A large portion of the love felt in any relationship is due to you reacting to being in their company with the feeling of love. Once you learn how to express with love creatively and more constantly, anyone else entering your life will be nothing more than a complement to experience these feelings of love you are feeling even more. Not to mention that if, for whatever reason, you break up and go your separate ways, you won't be completely dependent on them as the only source to feel more love in your life.

Let us continue together on this journey of self-discovery as I begin to touch just the tip of the iceberg of how every second of your life can start becoming an indescribable bliss if you choose it to be.

Integrate your senses with love

So, now we begin to dive into the mindfulness section of the book.

Let us look now at our lives and our daily experiences in how we experience life. It is through our senses: with what we see, what we hear, what we smell and taste, and what we touch and feel.

I will go through all of the senses now and add some exercises to help you cultivate a tremendous momentum to experience them more with love.

I ask you to experiment with all five senses at first. You might find one or two of the senses to be your strongest to start with. Use the senses you are strongest with to help support the other senses until they all start working together and compounding the experiences you begin having in life.

In time, all your senses will work together as you experience moments in life that will send you into the most profound moments of bliss.

Once you get this, life in itself becomes so much more magical.

See with love

Let us focus on our vision first and try to see the world around us through the lens of love.

The greatest gift we have to help us practice this is through nature.

Next time you have a second to stop, sit down and smell the roses, take a moment and sit down and start looking at the trees and grass around you, sending love through your eyes.

Breathe the experience in, and then try to look a little deeper.

If you are struggling to send and receive love through your eyes admiring the perfection in nature, you may have to go back to your list of things you love doing in the previous chapter. List them in your mind and recall your memories of doing them to kindle the feeling of love in your heart. Fan the fire of love in your heart, and then pass the torch of love to everything around you.

Whether it is martial arts, painting, walking on the beach, or any hobby, whatever it is, think about it. The feelings of love tied to doing those activities will start to surface in you.

If this doesn't work for you, go through one of your favorite meditations in this book so far, meditating until you slow down your thoughts and feelings, then open your eyes, looking at nothing but nature around you.

The next step is to use the love you are feeling and direct it to everything around you while you look at it. That fire of love extends from your heart to your eyes and to whatever it is you focus on.

Take three to five minutes to absorb all of nature around you, and watch how time starts slowing down.

You may see birds or butterflies, a beetle or bug may surface, or even just the soft breeze of wind on your cheek, or the sun's warmth that heats up and charge your back.

Look up to the sky and look at the clouds, seeing the contrast in colors.

Breathe in the experience.

Now take another breath in, this time with love.

Thank your heart and absorb this moment. That moment becomes like a jewel to you—a jewel to keep in the treasure chest of your heart.

You can repeat this at sunset— observing the peach and golden tones in the sky.

Becoming one with the golden disc of the sun slowly descending down until it falls out of sight.

Absorb every color of the purple hues that follow from here as the horizon bridges from day to night.

And then you can begin focusing on the stars at night.

Nature is just one angle you can use to really build this new way of sensing and experiencing things you see with love.

You can also look at everyone around you with love.

When I see that same shining white pearl within my heart as being within the hearts of others, I see myself in them. It helps me look beyond a person's outer trappings and more to their inner essence. Try not to gaze to long though, as you may send them the wrong message!

If you are reading my book, try sending love through your eyes to the words on the page. If you are listening to me speaking, whatever it is your doing or looking at right now, try sending love into what you are looking at.

If you really want to, get lost in this.

These exercises are to help you start experiencing it, but we are using our sense of vision all the time. You can focus on your morning coffee cup as you wake up and look at it between sips, sending it love. You can do this with anything: your computer screen as it's booting up. Try it with animals and watch how they react. You are processing what you see all day. Why not work towards adding love to every one of those moments?

Listen with love

In an earlier chapter, I shared the idea of listening gracefully with your mind free and empty from any thoughts or opinions.

Once we start listening in this manner with constancy, we begin retraining ourselves to live life with a constant empty mind. Listening gracefully becomes the bridge we cross to enter into an empty mind. It is also an active meditation, as we become one-pointed with our focus on what is happening completely outside of us through the sense of listening.

I hope you have been integrating this into your days like I suggested. If not, I encourage you to do so.

Let us continue listening like this, but now practice putting more love into the action of listening, adding the feeling of love as the reaction when hearing sounds around us, both loud and gentle, and most importantly, falling in love with the sound of silence. Let us listen deeper when we hear the sound of silence as if we are listening to the sound of love.

Listening to a loved one or anyone speaking to you in this state is incredible as well; as you stay empty listening to them with love, its like you can almost feel their heart and soul within the sound of their words as they speak to you.

Sitting outside and listening with closed eyes to the sounds around you is another way to get lost in love.

Take moments out of your day to do this often. Also, while you are facing the world and interacting with others.

As this love builds, the jewels you now hold in your heart will melt even the coldest walls in others if you listen to them speak and listen only with love.

Next to our vision, we are always listening. Those moments of silence make us listen even deeper and focus more on listening. Just as I have mentioned in how only listening can break through any racing mind or uncomfortable emotion, once you build this sense of listening up with love and add it into action, nothing will be able to steal your harmony.

Smell with love

Before you eat a meal, take a second to breath in through your nose and search for the smells the food you have prepared is giving.

When you leave outside walking to your car in the morning, breathe in through your nose.

Can you smell the flowers or other scents from nature outside?

It may seem like this sense seems less common throughout the day, but it is a constant sense we can be experiencing, provided we are breathing in through our nose; remember that.

When you are listening, and you can't hear anything, your senses become more sensitive. When we breathe deeply through our nose, we can still use our sense of smell, searching for smells even if we can't smell anything.

This sense of smell needs to be driven by love to help compound our daily experiences, as the key is to layer the senses into experiences we receive daily. For example, when you witness a moving scene of nature, like seeing birds chirping in trees at sunset. Our eyes see the birds, and they draw us into their world. We then hear their chirping conversation, which takes us even more into the moment. After admiring the experience for a moment, if you breathe in through your nose and are greeted by the smell of the flowers blooming on the tree, it adds even another layer to the experience, compounding the amount of love felt within that simple experience.

Smelling is another sense you can get lost in.

Taste with love

Whenever you drink or eat, it is an experience where we can also cultivate more love. If you eat in front of the television or eat while watching YouTube or scrolling through your mobile phone, stop it now!

Why would you let the monkey mind steal this sacred moment from you?

To start building love within this sense, try chewing your food at half the speed you usually do, and as you chew, imagine all of the cosmos breaking down that food with your saliva. Try to keep chewing on the food until it starts dissolving by itself before swallowing it and feeling the difference in how more nourishing it is.

This can also be practiced while drinking; instead of gulping your drink down, mix a mouthful around your mouth to mix it with your saliva while you swallow. Even drinking water alone without a taste can also be given the same action. Get creative with it. When I am drinking a glass of water, I often picture that star I spoke of in a previous meditation shining above me, releasing a waterfall into my being that I ingest through drinking the glass of water.

You can also see the same waterfall above you coming from that secret star while you are standing in the shower, they say our skin is like a massive tongue and can absorb water touching it. This is something for you to try yourself. The more you practice having fun with this, the more you'll experiment and come up with creative ideas to stay in the cycles of love.

Once you have practiced adding love to the action of chewing and breaking down food with your saliva, you can then begin to experiment with touching the top of the roof of your mouth with your tongue throughout the day and feel this sense of taste in action even though you're not eating.

Touch with love

It is one of my favorites and one I often get lost in.

Try this exercise right now: Look for a physical object, something small and light that you can hold in one hand but solid— like a pen or something.

Now, hold it in your hand before you, with your thumb or index finger free, and touch it slowly, easing pressure into it slowly. Try to feel the sensation as your thumb or finger makes contact with the object, monitoring the feeling as you gradually increase the pressure of your touch.

Stop and do it again, trying to put more love into the action.

Now, try and repeat this exercise again. This time, we will

try and do all our fingers and thumbs simultaneously, either slowly clenching into a fist or holding something or resting our hands on a desk or bench like we're playing the piano. Try this for a couple of times and see if you notice anything different. Now your attention is drawn to it; any action with your hands today and from now on can be done with this thought in mind. It's funny when you start observing how much we do with our hands but never really notice it, mostly because we rely on our unconscious to do everything.

You can keep a pen or something small in your pocket for the next couple of days to give you a toy to fidget with if you choose, experimenting with slowly loving it as you touch it to begin building this sense to another level.

Imagine yourself driving a car holding the steering wheel, and integrating love into the action. Your drive home from work could completely take a new direction if you merged this into it.

How many hours do we spend driving a week?

Even holding your mobile phone in your hands, writing text messages, and sending emails becomes something else so long as you link your senses to it.

Another thing is our sense of touch isn't limited to our hands, but also our feet.

That first barefoot step out of bed in the morning is your first point of contact with the ground beneath you. If you pause for a second before jumping out of bed in the morning and start to anticipate that first step for the day as being a magical moment, sending love through your feet to the ground beneath you like we have done in the earlier exercise with the pen or object, then stand up as tall as you can with both feet anchored to the ground. After doing that, connect to your center then take a deep breath through your nose.

What have you just done?

You've set yourself up to have a perfect day. Just as long as you can stay connected and centered through every moment.

Are you starting to see things come together at all?

This is the ultimate goal of what we are trying to achieve through this book. A perfect day, every day. And how can we turn a day around in a matter of minutes when it isn't going in the right direction?

So I need to ask how much energy you are putting into your first step?

Every footstep can have the same intent and expression as what we put into our sense of touch through our hands. Experiment with it for a bit and see if it works for you. Imagine stepping through puddles of water and trying not to make any ripples in the water; that's one way to become more mindful of your step immediately. This worked for me when I was working in this area of my world. From there, I became more mindful of not being so heavy with my steps and would self-correct whenever I caught myself dumping my weight onto my feet. Even simply thinking further than your feet to the ground beneath your feet helps in so many ways. If you are not moving, take a second to connect with the ground under you, then scan your feet, legs and body quickly as being supported by that. Just by walking and feeling both the ground and your feet and the sensation of the bottom of your foot (even with shoes on) as it makes contact with the ground. Once you draw your attention to it and start feeling each step as you touch the ground, it becomes easy to apply more and more love into every step you take.

Walking around like this makes life so much more fun. I love to watch my youngest daughter try and walk on the cracks of the cement and paving when we are walking to the shops as she plays the game 'the floor is lava', as well as watching her splash her feet in puddles when it's been raining.

Remember as a child in how much fun you had while walking?

Do you think it was because you were putting your full attention into every step?

You can have so much fun if you have the right attitude and try adding the keys to this chapter into your daily life. Even if you can't feel or add the love to your senses immediately, if you are conscious of and monitoring these daily actions you do and enjoy watching them, the love will build and start to snowball.

It continues to get more and more intense, taking you into a better space the more you pursue experiencing this.

Let's picture it when you are cooking and preparing a meal. The love that's put into the food for yourself or those who eat it?

I used to love my mother's cooking, as I knew it was one of her love languages in how she would show her love for me.

Even when you open a door and grasp the door handle to unlock it. Try doing the action twice as slowly and watch how aware you are of everything and how easy it is to add more expression to this simple action.

You can do this with any action—typing the keys on your computer, writing with a pen—and if you work with your hands, try adding love through your hands as you work and witness how much more enjoyable it becomes and how the days stop dragging on so much. Most people work a minimum of 40 hours per week. If you subtract the hours you sleep at night, you spend more time at work than at home.

Why not experiment with this to try and have more fun while working?

You'll love your work when you work with love, and the sense of love will start working for you.

First example of all your senses in action

Try having fun next time you prepare a meal and treat it like a ritual. Let's say you are chopping vegetables for a stir fry. Hold the knife you are cutting with and send love as you grip the handle of the knife.

As you slice the vegetables, drive into the action of cutting the vegetables with love. Be focused on your actions; we don't want you to lose a finger in the process!

Then pick up the prepped food with love and drop it into the frying pan at half speed, so you can really monitor the movements you are doing.

Moving at half speed gives us more time to observe everything that is going on and helps us add more love into our actions.

You can do this while making anything to eat or drink:

· Building a sandwich
· Making a coffee or tea
· Making a bowl of cereal
· Grilling food outside on the barbecue

Once you have practiced this and have love flowing through your sense of touch into your cooking and preparing food, what about if you put on one of your favorite songs to play in the background?

Now you can listen to the music with love while you are putting love into the sense of touch as you prepare your food.

This is when you can start compounding love into the whole experience:

- Putting love into your touch as you prepare the meal
- Listening to the music in the background with love or of the sounds being made around you
- Looking at everything you are doing, sending love through your eyes
- Smelling the aromas of the food with love as its cooking
- While breathing in through your nose and smelling the food, quench your mouth, imagining your already tasting the meal. Often, you can taste the food by smelling it, depending on the meal.

Once you integrate all your senses to the level, they start working together to express love as a team. You can also experiment by adding deeper breaths of love in through your nose to add another level again.

I hope you have fun with this.

Second example of all the senses in action

Next time you go on a fitness walk, walk the dog, or even walk to the shop, as you are walking, try to gently touch your thumb and index fingertip together, just enough to kindle a sensory response, then add love to the sense of touch you are feeling.

- Now, draw your attention to your feet, feeling the bottom of your feet pushing against the soles of your shoes with each step you take
- Extend that love from your feet into the ground below you and focus on each step until you are connected to the ground and can sense it beneath you
- Once you have the sense in your steps switched on, start looking around at nature around you, sending love through your vision at what you see.
- Try smiling as well. It makes sending love through the eyes easier while you are smiling. You can think that when you smile, pull back your shoulders just an inch and see your chest smiling also
- Breath in through your nose and search for any smells around you
- Listen with your ears and search to see if you can hear anything

If you can't smell or hear anything, being unable to smell or hear anything means your senses will focus and amplify even stronger, meaning even more love will follow.

Once you have every sense of working together to express love, you can work on adding the layer of breathing in through the nose deeply with love still searching for smells around you.

After practicing this several times, the moment you begin walking, your feet walking will start turning everything on automatically, bringing you into that zone immediately. Practice this, and see for yourself.

These two examples give you an outline for anything. Mopping the floor, doing the dishes, or doing any other activity—and how can you introduce every sense into the experience individually until they all start working together.

This multiplies the more you practice it.

My personal testimony: because I have practiced this and spent a lot of time in this state, spending time sending love through my senses, any time that I am out in public, at work or whenever now, all I have to do is gently touch my thumb onto my index fingertip, and it feels like two electrical wires are touching, which lights me up and brings me immediately into this state of being able to observe everything around me with all my senses simultaneously, ready to start expressing love into everything around me. I am human, just like you, which means anyone can achieve this if they invest enough time practicing and pursuing it.

This is only touching the tip of the iceberg of what can be achieved through practicing this, and I will continue to explore this more.

Reflective exercise: your sacred mealtime

I want you to choose one meal today to enjoy and be completely present.

Make sure you leave your phone in another room, then sit down with your meal free from distractions at the table.

Rather than eating it immediately, take a moment to look at it. Anticipate how good it is about to taste, how grateful you feel to have food in front of you, and how much you are about to enjoy eating it. Then, try to dissect the meal and determine all its ingredients and how much each different ingredient will nourish your body.

Now, pick your cutlery up slowly at 50% speed, as you usually would, feeling the sensation of love pass through your hands as you hold your knife and fork in your hands. Slowly spike the food with the fork, and rest the knife on top of the meal before you cut through it slowly with grace.

Please note: *If you don't have cutlery, if you're eating out or eating take away. You can either take a moment holding it in your hands before biting into it, or take your time unwrapping it at half the speed you usually would.*

Still moving at a 50% speed to usual, raise the first bite of food to your mouth. Make sure not to chew it immediately, and take a second to taste it before you start chewing.

Observe how your mouth starts producing saliva as you chew it, and how important the saliva is in breaking down the food you are chewing on. Start experimenting with adding more love into the movement of your jaw while chewing the food. See the action of you chewing and the saliva in your mouth, filling the food, turning it into a perfect energy for your body.

Keep chewing and chewing, and notice the change in taste and texture of the food. Then, swallow the food and try to trace it moving down into your stomach.

Repeat this with every bite until the meal is finished, and try to overflow all of your senses with love throughout the meal until it's finished. Look to the plate before you, sending love through your eyes, reflecting on the meal's completion. You can even put your hands on your stomach as if your hands were sending love through your hands to the meal in your stomach for a minute.

You should be in the most incredible space at the end of the meal.

Spend the next hour reflecting on how nourishing the meal

was for your body.

Meditation exercise: enter the secret chamber of your heart

For this meditation, let us find a place where we feel comfortable, sitting or lying. It doesn't matter.

Get comfortable, and run a few breaths through the nose into the white pearl, your spiritual center.

Slowly lead yourself into that state of meditation.

Now, with your index and middle finger on your right hand, reach across your chest and place it firmly on the left-hand side around the middle of your ribs, searching around for the pulse of your heartbeat. Be patient, as it may take some time to pick it up.

Once you find your heartbeat, close your eyes and focus on the feeling of your heartbeat through your fingers.

Now, see a smaller version of yourself about the size of your thumb, clothed in white, running up a wide, white spiral staircase until you reach two massive wooden doors.

You push them open walking into a large room with a white marble stone floor and see a bright star in the center of the room before you, pulsing to the rhythm of your heartbeat.

The rays of light coming from the bright star fill the room.

You kneel down, and sit down in front of it and feel completely comfortable staring into it.

Your eyes start adjusting to the star's brightness, and you see colors start to filter through as the intensity of the light dims a little.

You start meditating upon this star which starts to look, more like a crystal ball. You look into it, seeing all of the cosmos.

You see the stars shining and meteorites flying past.

This is a crystal ball of cosmic consciousness right within your heart.

Within the universe, within this crystal ball of cosmic consciousness, you look further, deeper, seeing the white fire core of this universe as being the source of all life.

You continue to meditate and gaze on this crystal ball, you start to see three plumes of flame pouring forth from it: A dazzling golden plume, a deep brilliant rose pink plume and a brilliant electric blue plume.

These sacred flames pulse simultaneously, dancing in unison to the pulse of your heartbeat you are feeling.

Joy fills your being as you watch this threefold flame pulsing to the rhythm of your heartbeat.

Now, breathe deeply through your nose and watch the three flames intensify in light, then blow out your breath through your mouth onto the flame.

It intensifies, and it moves with your breath.

You feel the love in this flame.

You feel the power in this flame.

You feel the wisdom in this flame.

This is your flame of life. The flame within your heart, to kindle daily with love and devotion.

Stay within this secret chamber for as long as you feel necessary, then open your eyes and return to.

Repeat this meditation again before you go to sleep once you get into bed.

Things to consider

The first time running through the exercise of a mindful meal is exaggerated for a reason: to help you add more love into the sequence of actions to complete the exercise of consuming this meal. After several times of doing it slow, you can pick up the speed, and you will notice a difference in how you eat prior to performing this exercise.

If you hit a plateau with the intensity of love you are experiencing down the track, I encourage you to go back to 50% speed with eating and the daily activities you're trying to do more mindfully to help you bring a greater force of love into your world.

After experimenting even a little with this, every meal becomes a magical moment for you, even while eating with others. Even while conversing with them, because you have retrained the ritual of eating for yourself, it becomes unconscious to eat in this manner.

On average, everyone eats two to three main meals a day. You owe it to yourself to have at least one sacred meal each day and really try to lose yourself in the moment.

This meditation on the secret chamber of your heart will work wonders for you if you are constant with it. I challenge you to try and perform this meditation daily, entering into that room and connecting with that crystal ball of cosmic consciousness, even if it is only for a minute or two. See what changes you start seeing in yourself after seven days of it.

With practice and constancy, often you'll open your eyes, still seeing yourself in that room within your heart in front of the flame. Once we get to this level, it is from here that you want to try and experiment with doing some simple tasks around the house while still paying your full attention to yourself in that secret chamber sitting before that flame.

If you can get this part, watch how quickly life will change for you.

All your daily problems in your life will start fading away, or you'll receive insights from within on how to resolve them quickly.

The personal projects you are working on will also become easier to complete.

This is your inner self.

Think about that for a second...

This may sound a little bizarre to some who are reading this, but if you put in the effort with this, you'll witness it for yourself.

Even after ten minutes of being active while still focused on being present within your heart before that flame, you'll start seeing all the benefits of meditation but it also starts taking things to another level.

The meditation gives a more accurate description, but even if you start with feeling the beat of your heart and that flame dancing and pulsing to the beat of your heart.

In time, you won't need to put your hand on your chest anymore to feel your heartbeat as you will feel this flame as the force beating your heart, giving you an even greater connection to life.

You can use this meditation as a visual aid to replace the shining white pearl in the earlier meditations in this book, almost like adding another layer if you choose.

You can even think of the shining white pearl as the crystal ball of cosmic consciousness mentioned in this meditation.

If it's your first time reading, still try to do what I am suggesting, but this can also be revisited if you choose if it's a little too much to grasp now.

8

The Key to Transformation: Embracing Love

Let's reflect on the keys I've shared with you so far...

Whenever you feel out of sorts now and need to settle your thoughts and emotions, you can regain your balance simply by taking a few deep breaths to the rhythm of eight counts. This technique is also so simple; it can be practiced anywhere: at work, in the supermarket, in the waiting room at the doctor's, or while you are out anywhere in public.

We've seen the impact of what multi-tasking and taking on too much can have on our minds and the weight it puts on our shoulders. We've also learned that by operating off a to-do list, we can become much more productive and manage our days with much more clarity.

We have also learned the power of listening gracefully in complete silence. Which is listening without any personal opinion and focusing only on absorbing everything around us.

I gave you the task to set multiple daily alarms on your phone, reminding you to reconnect and then focus on listening; if you have done this, you should feel incredibly comfortable and content with staying in the space of only listening and absorbing everything around you.

Having both the breathing and listening exercises up your sleeve to use when needed are your greatest tools for re-aligning yourself without closing your eyes and meditating.

We have also explored the basic methodology of meditation and how to overcome the monkey mind, giving you several different meditations to explore and practice. I hope that at least one or two will resonate with you and that you will choose to make them your own.

Next, we explored self-correction and how to divide ourselves into four different quadrants to take a faster approach to identify, self-correct, and re-align our psyches.

We then explored the importance of becoming childlike and viewing the world around us with more simplicity, which is the first step to becoming more mindful. We then introduced the idea of seeing love in a whole new perspective as a creative force to help fuel our everyday actions.

Lastly, we also went through multiple ways to integrate more love into our five senses to help improve our daily experiences in life by being more mindful and in the moment.

Repetition enables retention.

Let us continue as I share more ideas with you on love.

The power of love

People have sung and preached about it, but the more you tune into love, the more you'll see its power. You may start seeing the wisdom in love, which can be seen clearly when you align with your heart before you make a decision to act on something.

I want you to start viewing love as a bucket of water—the only thing you need to extinguish any fire in your world, for love is a force that can be used to help resolve any problem you're facing.

I'm not saying all we have to do is smile and open our hearts, then abracadabra! All of a sudden, every problem in our world will disappear.

Not at all.

What I mean is once you align your feelings to love, you align yourself to this greater universal force and then govern this force around you to help you with everything you do.

We have to start thinking bigger for a second here...

Once you've aligned yourself with this force of love, you can add it to any issue you face. Now you have this force of love assisting you to restore things back into balance, as love naturally corrects everything and restores alignment.

Think of when you are swimming in the ocean at the beach: swimming over waves is more of a challenge when the only progress you make towards the direction you are heading is from your own movements, however, once you turn around and swim with the currents of the ocean, not only does it make life easier, you find moments where the waves lift you up and start carrying you.

Once we start co-creating with love, you will see your swimming with the waves and not against them.

You can even imagine an imaginary ocean around you if it helps you to see this force in motion, so when you send love in any direction, there are waves travelling from around you with your heart in the direction love's sent.

Be careful not to think you're the one doing this; you are not. We have to surrender ourselves completely first. Just as a drop of water dissolves into the ocean before it starts moving with something greater.

If you have been practicing the exercises I have shared on love so far in the earlier chapters, we will be able to work so much more closely together as we continue through the pages ahead.

If you have yet to practice the exercises and are hooked on reading the book, that is awesome; keep going; just remember to go back and go through each chapter again, completing the reflections and meditations and adding the tools shared to your days to really integrate everything I am speaking of into your world.

Even just reading this book will benefit you immensely, so you do you. This is your book now. Just buckle up, because it will start getting a little more intense as we have just crossed the book's halfway mark.

Seeing love as light

If anyone reading these words is still finding it hard to connect to the essence of love or sense the feeling of love within themselves, as said earlier, if you are feeling peace, that peace is love.

You can also experiment a little and replace trying to sense the feeling of love with seeing this love as light, which it is in a sense.

For example, try seeing your heart as a light bulb right now and turn up the imaginary dimmer switch in front of you to make the room or area you're in brighter and brighter for a second if you can.

Stop reading for a second and try it.

You could also see your eyes as being like two torches, shining beams of love into whatever it is you're looking at. Then play around with sending whatever it is you are looking at with love and light, or even start filling the spaces within every atom of the object with light and see it shining brighter and brighter with intensity.

You could also experiment with adding light to your senses, such as transferring light through your sense of touch and breathing in light as you use your sense of smell.

When I say light, I mean seeing a diamond-white light, like the sun shining in the middle of the day or even starlight to mix it up.

Use your imagination with this, as everyone is different. Some people are intuitive with their feelings, whereas others are more visual. Anyone struggling to tune into love with their feelings, perhaps try this.

This is also ideal for anyone who has read through the book more than once and wants to try something new.

It may sound a little mystical, but even alchemists must understand how to govern light before they can precipitate.

Either way, you choose to identify love, remember it flows from the heart.

Keep your heart open always

Our hearts are our point of contact with those higher planes just above and beyond the physical. If we keep our attention on that space we have reached through our peaks in meditation and hold our hearts open to it, our hearts become a magical portal in a sense.

The light from those higher planes begins shining through

us, into everything we come in contact with. If you have been meditating on that shining white pearl as I have been suggesting, this will come to you a lot quicker. It doesn't matter whether you have been meditating on your secret star, your tropical beach, or the secret chamber, by entering into your heart and leaving your outer awareness behind you, entering the heart is the doorway that will lead you into higher levels of consciousness.

Even if you are unable to sense or see these higher realms in your meditating within your heart, I assure you, they are there. Nonetheless, don't try to force the process by pushing yourself up into those inner levels in heart, forcing your way up, that will get you nowhere. More so, know these higher levels of formlessness exist, accepting that their there, understanding that this and everything within you will unfold for you when you're ready.

Until then, I want you to see your heart as a window or a lattice with the light from these higher octaves light shining through. Once you become comfortable seeing this, you can then begin experimenting with opening every cell of your body to let the light shine through you and bless the outer world around you. This visualization in itself will help you to hold your attention on those higher planes more as well.

Our atoms are a window into something bigger

When you visualize an illustration of an atom, you see the atom as the nucleus with all these electrons orbiting around it.

Imagine our solar system now; you see the sun in the center, surrounded by the planets of this solar system orbiting around it...

Can you see any resemblance?

Surely, we must be more than just this clump of flesh we call our bodies.

Now, just to add a little more zen to the mix, draw your attention to your body and zoom in your focus as we ponder on these questions?

- *Does every atom in our being contain a solar system with planets of its own?*
- *Does this make us part of both the microcosm and macrocosm?*
- *If so, is the space of our solar system the exact same size of the space within every individual atom in our body?*

Talk about Big Bang theory!

I am not asking for an answer on this; I just ask you to ponder it for a bit; that opens our minds to a sense of expansiveness similar to meditation, which tells me that I am onto something here.

I am bringing your attention to these added dimensions within your heart, as this is where you'll find your inner self, for once you find them, you'll never look back. Then everything you say, everything you do, will come from and be be guided from that level within.

Put in the work I have mapped out for you, I promise you it's worth it.

Taking love to the next level

As you build this connection and flow more with the currents of life, you'll find whatever you are focused on, this love you've attuned to will envelope it. If it's a good thing in your world, the currents of love will amplify it, or if it's a problem you are wrestling with, the currents of love will help consume and correct it.

The good things in your world don't need any guidance, let's focus on resolving the negatives first so all you are left with is the good.

If you facing someone hostile or angry at you for whatever reason, simple. All you have to do is empty yourself and surrender into your center, listen to them, let them speak, and hear them out. It's fire versus water now: nothing beats love.

If you have been practicing integrating love with your senses, this is where the magic starts...

- You've emptied yourself, meaning your heart is now trans-ferring that light from both your inner self and the highest levels of your heart.
- You're looking at them and transferring love to them through your vision; that's right, this is happening always at all times and unconsciously now.
- You are listening with love, absorbing whatever they are throwing at you, and enveloping them in the love around them at the same time.
- By surrendering into your centre, there's even a greater momentum of love around you, working with you and helping you to achieve your desired goal.

Try this: *if you start to visualize and see the fiery white pearl within their heart as you are looking at them, and speak to that pearl when you speak to them, another level opens again.*

You see how compounding the senses in the previous chapters adds a compound effect to everything you do?

Even the hardest of hearts have to surrender to love.

If they keep going, keep your poise; no one is going to steal your thunder. As long as you are calm and respond from your center, and not their center, or their anger they are dishing out into the world, they will have to calm down. There are only so many lit matches you can throw into a bucket of water, expecting a fire to start before giving up.

In time, just being in a room with others and your Presence (with a capital P) will do so much. Even without you opening your mouth and saying a word.

Please note: I am talking about irate work colleagues, customers, friends, family members and so on. If you have someone holding a knife asking you to give them your wallet, don't just smile at them, look into their eyes and envelop them in love; use your instincts or give them your wallet!

Surrender to love

If you are facing a problem, you need to resolve, stop and surrender into your center, admitting it's got you, and ask yourself what you need to do to fix it. After asking yourself the question, focus your attention on the problem and love it. That's right, love it! Like you are giving it a big hug and want everything to get better. Applying this process becomes much more automated after two or three times, meaning you don't have to include the hug in the sequence unless you choose to.

By surrendering to this issue, you allow the currents of life to step in and help. It also turns it into an active meditation, as you love the problem and then start addressing the issue while in a state of grace, and this universal force steps in to serve you, which often works through others around you.

It is an awesome experience once you start seeing it in motion.

Try this at least a couple of times and experiment for your-self.

I often either get an immediate answer from the soft prompting of my heart, giving me the direct answer of what to do, or I'll be shown the outcome clearly and start taking the steps needed to take and it's like the force of love around me starts guiding me through everything and walking with me.

Once the issue is resolved, time and time again I am always shown that love was the answer. Or, I see how, just by sending love into the issue, it's like someone or something comes in to help and assist. It's almost like sending love towards the problem that has attracted the answer to the problem, like in the book 'The Secret'; I guess in this instance, the secret is love.

Love is forgiving

If you have someone who is close to you angry with you for something you have done, it doesn't matter who is in the wrong, you or them; send them love, and keep sending them love until the walls dissolve. They will come around, or you'll be prompted when it's the correct time for you to make the move to initiate contact. This also applies if you have been hurt by someone for something they did to you. As hard as it is to hear, let the love in your heart flow into the situation, forgive them and move on. One of the worst things someone can do is go to bed with a heavy heart.

If someone has done something bad to you, I'm not saying not to gradually move them out of your life or cut them out completely; that is your decision.

I speak of surrendering to all the baggage and negative emotions tied to holding onto things. I spoke briefly about how our emotional body is like water; in holding that thought, would you rather live life as a glass of water or a glass of mud?

Just move on, learn from it, and draw your attention to the twenty other awesome things that are happening in your life right now.

It's that easy!

One or two breaths, reconnect, turn on your senses and bang, you're back on top. Let's close the gap between who we were and who we are becoming and close it quickly.

You can still love any problem from a distance, and keep sending it love if needed.

Love is your friend

When I first introduced the topic of love, I described it as being the correct frequency to align our emotions with as we explored together in how to express with it.

Then we explored flowing with it even more, when we started aligning our senses to love. By attuning to this creative force and layering it into our everyday experiences, through our senses, now we have become co-creators with love.

In this chapter, we have now begun to explore the thought of an invisible ocean of love around us, that once we surrender to it, we can then govern it more with our hearts, helping us consume complex situations and resolving them.

Once you start experimenting with governing love at this level, it becomes magical. You start to see love as more than just a feeling or force, but more, an impersonal personality. Standing beside you, ready to serve and help when needed.

I'll leave you with that thought in love and see if it takes form for you.

Let us continue to practice acting and reacting with love and begin to experiment with adding love to all those difficult situations we face daily and, more importantly, to all the good things happening in our lives as well.

For instance, if your partner is on their way home from work after a long day, and you keep your hearts attention on them, that soft force will surround them and comfort them their whole drive home. When they open the front door, notice how much their faces light up when they see you.

The more you let go and let love lead, the more effortless things become. Observe it as the force leading everything and everyone around you and witness it for yourself.

All you need to do is surrender and let go of the desire to control the world around you and put your desire into understanding love.

Rekindling the feeling of love

A couple of chapters back, I asked you to write down several tasks you love doing and think about doing them as an exercise to help rekindle positive feelings within yourself.

How did you go with it?

Did it help you tune into the feeling of love?

This is an important task, and one I want you to try again as we go through another exercise.

Think of that hobby or activity you look forward to doing and love for a second. Picture yourself doing it, whether in memory or as you are doing it, to rekindle those positive emotions you link to doing that.

If you are struggling with this, close your eyes and meditate for a minute or two, so you are completely centered and switched on.

Remember that exercise where we tuned into the radio station?

This time, we are going to think of a dimmer switch lighting a room, grab that imaginary dial in front of us and try to turn that feeling of love up brighter and more intense.

- *Can you see the love in your heart lighting up the room and becoming brighter and more intense?*

Now pause for a second holding onto that feeling of love lighting up the room around you...

- *Can you enter into that love any deeper?*
- *Can you empty your thoughts like in meditation and listen for any sound to that feeling of love you are feeling?*
- *Can you let go of everything and surrender deeper into the ocean of love around you?*

Attune every one of your senses and your breathing now into expressing this love, then see the love as almost spherical, surrounding you.

Let's try and make it bigger...

If this is hard for you to see, use your breaths like you are blowing up a balloon of love around you, breathing in through your nose and breathing out slowly, which is expanding the sphere around you like a balloon, growing bigger and bigger with each breath.

· *As you look at this love around you now, can you feel what's behind the love you are feeling?*

Run through this exercise of reflective questions four or five times at least if you want to level up your peak experiences with love.

Once you get to the peak of the feelings experiencing love, try to hold it at that level, breathing in and out to fan the flame of love, increasing the intensity of your feelings even more.

Every time you do this, the peak of the experience becomes your new benchmark, which will take your day-to-day experiences to an even deeper and more meaningful level.

Every positive feeling originates from love

There is love in peace, there is love in joy, there is love in gratitude, and there is love in faith. Love can be seen as a universal energy that divides into different spectrums, like when you hold a crystal up to the sunlight and the rainbow colors shine through. With this deeper connection to life we have built through entering into our heart, we start to learn how to create from a higher place.

For example, feel that love shining brightly within your heart like the noonday sun. It feels warm and comforting, you may even feel your secret star shining above you too.

Now see the warm rays shine and extend towards your solar plexus, which is the bottom of your rib cage and just above your abdominals.

This area of the solar plexus we are focusing on is where we hold our emotions. When love descends to this level of our being it is expressed through our emotions and takes on more of the form of water. Picture a crystal clear pond as you look at this area of yourself.

Can you feel the water?

Lean to one side and imagine it creating ripples in the pond.

Now, lean the other way and do the same thing.

When you see a pebble dropped into a still pond, you see the ripples of water follow; you can almost see the same ripples of water flowing out to the world around you from all angles. Take just one minute to feel those water ripples flow out from your solar plexus in all directions.

Before you, behind you, to the left and right, your awareness expands with the rings as they travel further and further away from you.

Ripples of water expand and flow out into everything around you.

See the ripples of water flowing out from your solar plexus as being purple-gold, like the colours of the front cover of this book.

Now feel the love of your heart flowing and connecting to your solar plexus, and then your solar plexus, turning its own dial and requalifying that love to transmit the waters of peace to everything around you.

Pause from reading for a second and take a moment to feel it for yourself.

Every time you see water from this moment on, I want you to take a second to recreate this visual I have shared with you. You will see your feeling world and the ripples of golden water you are visualizing tune in with the water you are looking at, like you are mirroring it, bringing you closer to a connection with the element of water.

Even when you see a glass of water in front of you on the table, or puddle on the road. This is only for a week or two until you start seeing water around you, and you don't need to focus on aligning with it; then, you can drop the exercise as you have successfully brought your body more into balance.

You can see how love creates peace, and that peace is an extension of that love. If you pursue to flow with love, so many more doors will open for you.

Visualizing the purple-gold water ripples is an incredible meditation for anyone wrestling with their emotions. Focusing on this for even several days will result in massive change.

Start with closing your eyes to see it, then practice opening your eyes and holding it and watch it become an active meditation that you can hold for as long as you like.

If you focus on this extension of love entering your solar plexus and flowing out into your world, it will add another dimension to your life. So much so that you will become an ambassador of peace, consuming those energies and emotions in others around you that you used to wrestle with.

Finding a greater love through service

When I started this journey, I didn't have the tools I am sharing with you in this book to help me overcome the flaws within myself.

I knew I needed and wanted to improve myself, but because I was so inundated by my own thoughts and feelings, I couldn't see the keys that were placed right in front of me.

I owe my victory and constancy in conquering self, through finding service.

Service to others and serving life.

That is, looking to help others with no desire for a reward or self-motivation. It teaches you so much about yourself, as we meditate to empty our minds, we also empty ourselves through service.

People often get lost in it as it is so liberating. This can be serving family, friends, loved ones, or even a work collegue having a hard day struggling.

You can find service through volunteering, your spiritual community, even your local area. Just search online 'volunteering' or 'voluntary work', and you should find something close to you.

If you make an effort to help someone today, you will be walking on clouds for hours after it. I challenge you to prove me wrong.

Helping a stranger or someone in need without them asking, lights them up. That moment when they look at you and are moved by your kindness, it is something that needs to be experienced to truly see.

Life gets so much easier too, like all the baggage in your world goes on hold and is put to the side.

If you are struggling in finding or feeling love, you will feel love through service. As long as you do it with kindness and try to give that person a better day than what they were previously experiencing.

This is what life is about. This is what we are here for.

Once you start getting the bug for it, you'll see people needing a hand loading things into their car, an older person physically struggling to hold a door open to walk through with their shopping, and you'll step in asking if they need a hand without even thinking.

Just don't get hurt if they reject your offer or refuse your help; that's just your ego that has no place in our world now. Some people have insecurities, it's just what it is; like the fear of being robbed, or being too prideful to admit they need a hand.

You may already be a person who helps those around you. Awesome.

It's a little different when you start your day looking for life to bring you an opportunity to help someone as a daily goal.

What sort of attitude do you think you are embodying?

What purple-gold ripples of water are you sending out into your world?

Service is one of the four points to love; if you start experimenting with this while studying this book, you will see everything you are chasing amplified, even though you are not doing it for self-gain.

We do it because it is the right thing to do.

Anyone can align themselves through meditation and feel and experience these incredible feelings in themselves, but it is the champions of this world who will make the effort to lift up everyone around them.

That's the way I see it, anyway. If I am launching up, I am taking everyone with me.

Try this for yourself. Go out and look to help someone today or tomorrow. It doesn't have to be too big of a task; just look for an opportunity to serve.

Be warned, though, that the reward of service is more service!

More and more opportunities may start to present themselves, you'll feel so much more joy in your life, and receive so much more love and support from everyone around you.

As they say, what goes around comes around.

You'll also meet the best people you can imagine. The kindest hearts you could ask for, all with the most incredible stories to share.

If you are struggling within yourself, service is your medicine on top of whatever it is you are already doing.

Go now, give back to life, and watch the waters settle within yourself.

Keep your senses fueled with love

Remember to take moments each day to kindle the flame of love behind every one of your senses.

I suggested the sacred meal exercise prior because we all need to eat every day, and if you have one sacred meal daily, you know you do it with constancy.

Any ritual you do weekly by yourself: mowing the lawn, playing the piano, doing your washing, practice compounding love into your senses.

After a week or two, you won't need to think about things as much, and the love will flow through unconsciously. Your vision, your listening, and your hands through your fingers will be transferring love into your world.

As a co-creator with love, you may notice that the words in your emails and SMS messages will be charged with your heart as you write them, and the SMS or email receiver will catch that love.

Think of this...

If someone is in a bad space, wrestling with their day, and

your SMS comes their way, and it lifts them up, sending their day in a different direction. Everyone around them in their circle of influence has been lifted, too.

These purple-gold ripples are still flowing out from you and reaching so many more people than you are now aware of.

That leads me to ask...

- *Are you still seeing those ripples of peace flowing from your solar plexus?*
- *Keep visualizing them, those ripples travelling out from you will help you in ways that words cannot explain.*

Every meal you cook now tastes so much better because it is nourished with love.

Washing the dishes and sweeping the floor are no longer chores because you've compounded your senses to make it a ritual of love.

People will light up listening to you speak because you come from a place they also desire to be.

Be humble, though; it's not you; it's love.

Life is constantly changing for all of us. How it changes now is up to you.

Reflection exercise: conversation with a loved one

I want you, sometime today or tomorrow, to have a conversation on the phone or face-to-face with a family member or loved one.

As you listen to them, ask some open questions to get them talking so your leading the conversation with questions, but they are the ones mainly speaking.

Now empty yourself entirely and listen to them talk.

If their voice is a little agitating at first, keep listening...

Keep listening with no thoughts of what you want to say next, breaking through into that space of peace.

Listen deeply—deeper than their voice.

Try to listen and feel their heart and soul speaking.

With your eyes still open, see yourself entering your heart and continue listening.

See the shining white pearl within, and listen from that place, your inner ear.

See the same shining white pearl within their hearts as well, and focus on that as the point they are speaking from.

Hold the conversation and watch it take on a new dimension.

Listen deeply, giving them your full attention and enveloping them with love.

This in itself is enough to take any everyday conversation to a deeper and more meaningful level, but if you want to have a little more fun, experiment.

Continue the conversation now asking yourself

- *By speaking to the shining white pearl within their hearts, and not their ego at level of the belly, can you lift their soul and spirit up to the level of the pearl to meet their inner self?*
- *Can you ask your inner self to ask their inner self what needs you need to say or share with them?*
- *Can you open your heart and center yourself, coming from the level of your inner self and speak to them with an added dimension of love?*

The more you hold your focus on the inner planes of consciousness within your being and try to speak from the level of your higher self, you'll find yourself saying the most incredible things you wouldn't usually say.

You may even hear their inner self speaking, too.

Meditation exercise: the white cloud

Firstly, let us still all the outer activity of the mind and body.

Focus on nothing but your breathing, fanning the white fire within the shining white pearl in your heart.

You see the three plumes of brilliant electric blue, dazzling golden yellow, and deep brilliant rose pink pulsing and dancing to the rhythm of your heartbeat; you sit in awe, observing them in all their beauty.

You start focusing on the pearl beneath the three dancing flames and see it becoming brighter and brighter, like starlight. This pearl within your heart becomes a cosmic magnet, drawing in a 'cosmic substance' that surrounds your physical body.

It feels comfortable.

You feel the connection to this dazzling white cloud surrounding you to the pearl within your heart.

Slowly breathe into the shining white pearl within your heart and see the white light within it get brighter as the cloud around you gets brighter simultaneously.

The more you look into the white pearl, the brighter this dazzling white cloud becomes till you can't see past it.

It begins forming the shape of an auric egg, and you surrender every cell in your body to become one with this cloud.

This dazzling white cloud of cosmic substance recharges the cells within your body.

By intensifying the light even more, the diamond-white light purges all of your cells, restoring the feeling of perfection.

It is healing.

You feel at one with this cloud, feeling complete comfort of being inside the gentle but strong arms of this cloud surrounding you.

When you feel the time is right, conclude your meditation and open your eyes.

You may wish to journal your experience.

Things to consider

Along with every reflection exercise in this book so far, the first time experimenting with it, it can seem like the most significant task.

Nonetheless, after three or four times, it does become effortless and feels more comfortable listening to someone speak from the inner recesses of your heart rather than your mind. You'll build more trust in asking your heart for answers rather than just flopping your chops mindlessly. In our mind, it often feels like we are saying the right thing when usually, it is not.

Holding your attention to the other person's heart and soul while speaking also lifts them to commune with you from a better space.

This means that before you even open your mouth, you've pulled them out of their turmoil and allowed them to see their issues better.

This meditation is incredible to give while retiring at night and about to fall asleep in bed. It builds momentum and helps you see that just as we can invoke this dazzling white cloud of cosmic substance to surround us, by focusing on that pearl within our hearts, we can also focus this cloud of 'cosmic substance' to surround any area we choose.

Get creative with it:

- You can visualize this cloud charging the walls of your house and home.
- you can see it surrounding people you interact with at home or work.
- You can charge your meals with this cloud before you eat.
- You can try surrounding your car in it if it won't start in the morning.

I can't guarantee that it will start your car!

Just suggest you be creative and have fun with it.

If you pursue this meditation and use it, at the closing of your meditation, send the energy you have invoked to help you complete your personal projects or areas in life you seek to change.

It can't hurt trying, for everything is energy.

9

Your Magic Mirror: Reflecting the Radiance of the Sun

We have made a lot of awesome progress on our journey so far. Now it's time for me to introduce you to a dear friend of mine. A friend who has helped me so much in discovering these inner truths in life.

That friend, believe it or not, is the sun.

That's right, the sun shining above us in the sky every day, lighting up the world for us that we are often ignoring as we go about our days.

Let us try and change this and become more mindfully connected to the sun as I share some interesting keys with you.

As I have been saying before, the ultimate aim is to have a sequence of tools assisting us to stay connected and in alignment with the inner parts of our being, and the sun shining above us is one of those things. For example, from your first step out of bed, your ritual of getting ready for work, stepping outside to be greeted by the outside trees and the welcoming fragrance of nature. From here, the search in the sky to see the suns' location is the next level from there, as it does so much more than we are aware of.

The sun is like nature; I have found through experimenting with using them both as anchor points to bring me back in alignment; this sounds bizarre, but I found the sun to start working with me and helping me in re-aligning myself. It's like it talks to me. Not with words, but more of an instant understanding and calling me to realign myself.

This chapter is titled 'The Magic Mirror' because that is what the sun is: a magic mirror. Like anything, though, it takes practice. If you are constantly practicing these exercises I am about to share, it will bring another level to your mindfulness and how you stay connected daily.

I also say, with so much love, the relationship I have built with the sun has become beyond physical, it has now become magical. I am in no way special or any different to you. I am writing this chapter because it's what a true friend would do. Everyone needs to know this. I ask you to remember this once you find this magic for yourself.

I am going to go deep into this one, so don't be overwhelmed if you are not following all of it; just read through and come for the ride with me, as I'll be taking you places with my words. Nonetheless, even if you take just two or three keys I share away with you and integrate spending moments with the sun into your daily schedule, everything I say will be understood by you so much faster.

Let us look back to ancient times: the Egyptians, Aztecs, Incans, and Ancient Greeks all saw the sun as a God. I firmly believe without a doubt, that it was because they were more heart-centered and felt a solid connection to the sun.

With what we have covered so far, we are already becoming more heart-centered. So, let us add another level to the heart, which is the center of our own universe.

Please note: I've used the examples of ancient civilizations to illustrate they saw more to the sun than what we do in modern times, I haven't said the sun is a God. I will say, though, that the sun is definitely the heart to something bigger or our next point of focus we need focus on to expand ourselves higher in consciousness.

After you read this chapter and practice the exercises I share, you may start to see it as well.

Start to mirror the warmth of the sun

The sun gives life to every plant on the planet. Only a handful of plants can survive in this world without sunlight. Regardless, of whether we look at this spiritually or scientifically, we can see the sun as the energy providing life to our planet. Or, to be a little more diplomatic, if you are in a particular discipline of faith, you could also look at the sun as being what your creator uses to give life to the planet.

Regardless of our view or standpoint, we have to be more mindful of the sun in our lives every day. The first step to doing this is to simply try going outside and stopping for a minute while the sun is shining to feel the sun's warmth.

This could be with your morning coffee or smoothie first thing, leaving a minute earlier for work, and taking a second to pause and absorb the rays of the sun before you get in your car. It could be through one of your breaks at work, or even by just being aware of the sun in the sky while you take a fitness walk or ride. If this is not possible, try to find the sun in the sky while driving in your car or travelling.

Once you find the sun in the sky, feel the warmth in its rays. Breathe in deeply through your nose and recenter yourself, then start mirroring it.

What I mean, is to copy that feeling of warmth you are feeling from the sun and try to feel it in your solar plexus.

Remember that point where we visualized the purple and gold ripples of water flowing out around us in all directions?

Can you still see that?

If not, start visualizing it for a moment. We are retraining ourselves to hold that with constancy.

If you are out in the sun, don't worry about it so much. Just feel the warmth of the sun filling the core of your solar plexus and surrender to feeling one with the sun as if your solar plexus were shining with it.

Now let's do the same thing, extending the feeling to our hearts. It is the exact same process as before, but copy the warmth of the sun, mirroring it with your heart. Then feel and see your heart shining its rays of warmth in exactly the same way as the sun to the world around you.

Think of a lizard on a rock.

Take a moment just absorb the sun to recharge yourself.

If you feel comfortable and confident with this, you can then experiment with entering through those wooden doors within your heart into that secret chamber, entering the shining white pearl, and traveling up into your secret star, feeling yourself entering within it, and then shining light into the world around you simultaneously in exactly the same way as the sun.

If you did this even once a day, you'd see massive change within yourself. Twice would be better, though, once in the morning and once in the afternoon.

See every sunrise and sunset as a daily gift

There is something magical about stopping to witness the sunrise or sunset. Personally, for me, the sunset is the one I am more likely to stop and work into my daily schedule. It has become a part of my evening ritual. Like a snowflake, no two sunsets have ever been the same, and everyone becomes better than the last. Even if it's just for 30 seconds to stop and admire the beauty, like it's a painting that has been painted just for you. I often compliment it and have taught my daughters to do the same thing.

Try it for three or four times, and watch how that time of the day when the colors in the sky starts to change, how your soul or spirit lights up to it, like your being called to admire it.

If you make time for this, it becomes an active meditation as well.

- You start seeing nature move with the sunset.
- You begin hearing the birds sing in praise like they are thanking the sun for the day.
- You begin feeling a sense of oneness as the world slowly transitions to night.

With the previous exercise of mirroring the sun, this becomes automatic and unconscious after a while. Where that is happening while you are observing the sunrise and sunset.

I often play this game in my heart, where I imagine the yellow, pink, and blue flames within my heart, the one I described in a previous meditation, as being the primary colors of paint on an artist's palette, and I mix and blend them to make the tones of peachy golden hues, sometimes even expanding my heart as if I were painting the picture I am seeing before me and even being empty of thought and absorbing it for a minute. Every time I merge the colors in the flame within my heart to the scene in the sky, it feels expansively incredible.

Pink and yellow make peach, and blue and pink make purple, if you see no purple in the sunset, remember the sky is still blue behind you.

This is the game I've made with myself to play with my inner child; you might find your own, or even play the game I just mentioned.

Have you ever heard of someone complaining they had to stop and watch a sunset?

I know I haven't.

Try it for yourself and see if it does anything for you or not.

Breathe in the sun

The more we start connecting with the sun daily, the more we'll start becoming more sensitive to it. Not just the warmth of the sun, but the love and light within it. Even the fire and spirit of it. Not to go too sideways with spooky shamanism, but it's possible you'll start to notice the light around you more that's lighting the day and being connected to the source it's coming from.

The breathing exercises I have shared with you so far continue to give them to re-center yourself and fanning the fire within the shining white pearl of your heart and the nucleus of every cell of your body. Now that we are a little more mindful of the light around us, let us add the light from the sun to the air we breathe. That bright white light—you see the sun when it is shining above during the zenith of the day; you see the air you breathe as shining in the same way.

You can visualize breathing in that sunlight and letting the sunlight fill and shine in every cell of your body. Anything that is not shining at that brightness we are seeing, imagine when you breathe out, you breathe that darkness, tension, or sickness out of you until you are free from it and then see the sunlight leaving you as you breathe out.

Once you've built a habit with this, the next step is to breathe that sunlight into the center of every cell of your body: your hands, arms, torso, feet, chest, and every part all at once. It takes some time to peripherally see this action, but once you do, you'll start to see the sunlight breathing through your cells as you breathe.

The next level after that, is to start seeing the light of the sun, shining above you and through you, shining through the center of every cell of your body like every cell of your body is a sun in itself shining at the same time as the sun.

The sun's light has more dimensions to it; nonetheless, at this stage, this is not important, let us focus on governing it and letting it flow through us.

See the sunlight in food

So many people in the world count the carbs and calories in their meals. If you are doing this yourself, continue to do so. In conjunction with that, why not measure the amount of sunlight held within the food?

I was experimenting with this one day, eating an apple outside, and found just by observing the light within the apple and biting and chewing it; I felt I was adding another level of nourishment, and there was more to the apple than before.

From there, I started experimenting with judging food and accessing it by the amount of sunlight within it or that was needed to grow it. More so, fruit, vegetables, nuts and foods grown from plants. For example, if you take a second before biting into an apple and hold it in your hands, looking at the light within it and the light needed to grow it, pause, then bite into it. I promise you, it will taste a hundred times better.

This doesn't mean I am eating a hundred percent healthy diet; I assure you I am not. We are all working towards something. This is just an added exercise I've had great success with, and the more you practice the prior exercises of mirroring and letting the sunlight flow through you, like love, you'll sense in time, that you can govern that light a little more.

After practicing this for a while, you can experiment with the imaginary dimmer switch we have been using with the exercises on love to increase the intensity of the light and love within the meal before you eat it. This makes the ritual of eating so much more awesome and fun. Just keep this private and to yourself when you're doing it, as others around you will think you are wacko if you try to explain what you're doing.

When the sun isn't shining

It's good to be optimistic, but there will not be cloudless days of sunshine every day. That's why we are diligent with mastering this while we can so that even when the sun isn't shining in view for us physically, we'll still have enough memories of using the sun where we won't need the visual warmth of the sun to guide us.

This teaches us so much about so many things in life:

- Te know what feeling at peace feels like, even when we are feeling turbulence around us and within our emotions.
- To know when our mind is racing, what it feels like when it isn't, and that it will settle in time.
- To know the outcome of a problem you are facing and to take action on the steps needed to reach the outcome you desire from that problem.

You get the gist.

Faith is so powerful and isn't just limited to religion. Faith is knowing that something is in action even when it isn't; then, by knowing that it is in action, your focus is on what has already happened, which actually often helps drive it to happen, as well as helps you to remain unshakable to react to the present.

Knowing the sun is still shining when the clouds covering it are raining is an example of this.

The sun is the heart of our solar system

Look at how the sun is located within the center of our universe, with the Earth and other planets rotating around it. We can see the similarity with an illustration of an atom, the atom being the sun, with the electrons being the planets surrounding the atom.

Since reading this book, we have been working on becoming more heart-centered and how our hearts are starting to become the center of our universe.

Every time we draw our energies and attention into our hearts, and re-align our creative energies that were being wasted in idle thought and unnecessary emotion, we start seeing those energies begin to lock onto one point within us, the shining white pearl.

Then once we enter within that shining white pearl, we experience an expansion in consciousness.

Now think of the sun as being identical to your heart, but the heart of our solar system.

With that now established, here is what I want you to try:

Picture the sun in the center of the sky shining at midday with its diamond white rays extending out on every angle.

See your heart as shining to it with the exact same light, and the sun as being a bigger version of your heart, then see yourself being drawn into the sun and then into the sun's white fire core, which is similar to the shining white pearl within the secret chamber of the sun.

While focusing on the feeling of the shining white pearl within the sun, feel the white fire within it as being identical to the shining white pearl within your own heart.

Now, entering into the sun's white fire core, you return to the inner recesses of your heart, with the shining white pearl and blue, yellow, and pink flame above it.

Are you still following me?

We've drawn our focus to the sun, travelling into it through our hearts, entered the shining white pearl of the sun, mirroring the feeling of it with the shining white fire pearl within our hearts and returning into the secret chamber of our hearts.

We need to weave this one more time, so stay with me.

Now, walk into and re-enter the shining white pearl within your heart, and see yourself flying or travelling through space to the sun and landing within the center of the sun.

It is not at all hot when there in the higher etheric levels of vibration.

This area in itself is an area to explore; what do you see?

You can explore this at a later time; for this exercise, we are entering into the white fire core of the sun, which is the same white fire core or shining white pearl within our hearts.

Now try mirroring the sun's white fire core with the shining white pearl within your heart again, returning to the inner recesses of your heart, you sit or kneel the shining white pearl before you within this white quartz floor room within your heart. You see the trinity of the flames beating above it: electric blue, golden yellow and brilliant rose pink. They are more personal now, you feel they are your source to life.

A launch pad to take you higher.

The white pearl beneath the flames glows like mid-day snow, lighting the room within your being. With this deeper connection you have with the sun, every time you focus on the shining white pearl within your heart, you are simultaneously present and focusing on the white fire core of the sun.

This point within your heart is your connection to every-thing.

I am sharing a very personal experience with you here, which I feel can be obtained by everyone. If you get lost reading this part, please re-read it four or five times until you can mentally paint the process so you can experiment with it from memory without the words in front of you. As every time you run through the visualization, you are weaving a bridge that will act like a magnet, drawing you up into the sun every time you enter the inner recesses of your heart.

The secret star within yourself

If this is your second time reading this, or if you have taken up the challenge I gave you to meditate on your secret star for 7 days straight, then this one is for you.

It is one thing to mirror the sun with your heart, but I believe there's so much more to be done here. After aligning yourself to feel the warmth of the sun within your heart and aligning yourself more to the sun, why not then enter within your heart and into the shining white pearl and see the three flames merge with the white fire from the pearl beneath and expand and launch you up the crystal chord into the secret star within yourself.

See yourself now looking through the level of this secret star and send needle-like rays of love from the secret start within yourself to the heart of the sun.

Can you feel love being sent back to you?

We don't love to receive; we love to give. Having said that, whatever we send out into the world comes back to us tenfold.

Does this bring you any closer to understanding how the sun fuels our planet?

Let us put science to the side for a second, and let us start investigating the science of spirit. The science to life. The science of being aligned to and with everything in this world and how much more we open ourselves to these greater concepts that just keep unfolding to us like layers of an onion, bringing us closer and closer to truth.

The secret star within the sun

Now we have aligned ourselves to the sun and entered within to the secret star within our hearts, sending love from our secret star to the heart of the sun; let us look and ponder on the thought of what if the sun had its own secret star?

Like a sun behind the sun, or within and above it?

What if after we enter into the white fire core of the sun, we start entering into higher levels of consciousness that are beyond this universe and bring us higher and higher into cosmic consciousness?

Just a thought ;)

Let us begin by holding our focus on the heart of the sun and white fire core within the center of the sun.

Now enter into the secret chamber of your heart by opening the big wooden doors and seeing the shining white pearl with the blue, yellow, and pink flames above it within the center of the room. You walk into the shining white pearl and travel, to the center of the sun and enter the white fire core of the sun.

This take you into an even deeper space of consciousness. You see a white spiral staircase shining brightly.

"Take my hand; I'll race you to the top!"

You start running up the stairs, travelling higher and higher into the greater levels of awareness. You look up and see a faint outline of a star at the top of the spiral staircase. It is surrounded by brilliant colors and you know you have to make it up there.

You continue running up the stairs for as long as you can; whether you make it to the top or not the first time is irrelevant. After descending back down the stairs, an added dimension to these inner planes begins to unfold.

Next time you begin climbing the stairs, not only does it reinforce things and make them clearer, but you also gradually climb higher and higher.

When you reach the top, remember... It is a secret.

There are certain jewels in life where nothing good comes

from sharing them with others, as it is your own personal experience that begins diluting the magic you experience while in these places of heart.

You will benefit from trying this for yourself. It is perfect to give as your bedtime meditation and continue running up those stairs until you drift off to sleep.

We can do this at any time now

You don't have to have your eyes closed and intently meditating to do this either. If you have been following my instructions and have been working on re-centering yourself with the 5 alarms every day from your phone, it should be easy for you to add the final step, which is to enter into the shining white pearl after re-centering and have the flames above the pearl expand and launch you, up into the level of your inner self and then the secret star above.

The freedom to go anywhere

With our focus on that portal to higher levels of consciousness once entering into that white fire core, who's to say we can't travel to where we want to go?

If you have travelled the world and you remember a special place, you have golden memories.

You remember what it looked like.

I mean, you walked and stepped on the ground there.

While we do this exercise, think of that place, and imagine that after entering the shining white pearl, you travel there on those higher etheric levels of formlessness and stand there like you were physically present, only a little higher in vibration.

145

Is this possible?

Is this the sort of freedom we were originally intended to have?

With open eyes as I am typing these words, I have simultaneously entered my within my heart, travelling to a special place around the world I remember. That's my special place, though, where is yours?

The more you practice this, and build it up, there will be a point where you can withdraw almost fully from where you are with your inner vision and focus on being more present in the place you've cast your vision to.

Just for some examples:

- *When you have a loved one sick in the hospital.*
- *Your children if they are struggling in school.*
- *Or if you are away from your family.*

Use your imagination with this one; you can become that angel in the room sending love.

Remember how much more you are beginning to govern love now from the previous chapters?

Imagine if you are constant with this and how much more you can help others in say 3 to 4 months from now?

Interesting thought to have, I assure you, though, this isn't fiction.

Raising into the sun

This visualization is an interesting one. I spent a lot of time focusing on that secret star above me, which I have and will recommend to anyone again. It was in the midst of the day, walking, aligning with everything around me, sending love through my heart and to the secret star above me as I saw it loving everything around me as well. To my surprise, I felt the sun above me doing exactly the same thing, like I was sending love and light into the world simultaneously with the sun. Once I accepted that I was doing exactly the same thing, I felt myself higher, as if my heart was the same size and the height of the sun, with my head and torso just above it.

There is a sense of expansiveness to this as if you are meditating but moving freely. After going within that shining white pearl, you have the freedom to do so much more than you can imagine.

After that moment, I feel a connection to the sun whenever I look at or connect with it.

I explained earlier in the secret star meditation: when you send love from your heart, your secret star is now shining love simultaneously with you. Well, now it's your heart, the secret star, and the sun shining love and light simultaneously, not at the level where explained that I expanded and my heart was at the height of the sun, but more of a oneness with all three.

I know now when I focus on someone or something, I am sending love in that direction and enveloping them in complete comfort, and that secret star and the sun are working with me as if there was an oneness to the sun, my secret star and heart.

And pretty soon, there will be a oneness to the sun, with your secret star, and your heart, if you choose to pursue this. Now you know this you are free to practice travelling up within your heart and into the secret star and keep raising to the level of the sun now as well if you choose.

Reflective exercise: mirror the sun

For the reflection and meditation exercises in this chapter, they will both be active exercises. Even if you have read this book more than once, doing these two exercises is recommended.

For the reflective exercise, I want you to take some time at lunch, or when you can see the sun in the center of the sky, and sit outside and absorb some rays from the sun.

Get yourself comfortable, and breathe in the warmth of the sun.

You can imagine breathing in the light of the sun, which invigorates your lungs, diffusing any tension throughout your body.

Center into your heart and place your hands on your solar plexus (the bottom of your rib cage).

Empty yourself, feeling the sun's warmth, tune into your feeling world and emotions and try to mirror and copy the same warmth you are feeling from the sun in your solar plexus.

Hold the feeling for 30 seconds to a minute. Focus on the feeling of warmth you are copying, and see if you can make it stronger.

This is not to make it stronger but more so you to train yourself to create the same feeling without the sun in the future.

If you need to breathe in and out with your diaphragm to release any tension in your stomach, do so. Continue mirroring the warmth and feeling of the sun until you feel one with it.

You can if you want to extend this warmth to flow out with the purple and gold ripples of water from your solar plexus.

Now raise your hands to the heart level and do the same exercise: feeling the sun's warmth, tuning your heart in to feel that same warmth; you should have the same feeling as the sun within your heart now.

Mirror the feeling of the sun within your heart and imagine it shining in exactly the same way.

Once you feel one with the sun, send a missile of love from your heart above you to the secret star above you and then continue all the way to the sun.

Imagine a thread of contact or crystal chord coming back to you from the sun as the sun then returns a missile of love back.

See your heart as an extension of the sun, with the warmth and love of the sun pouring down this crystal chord and into your heart and the world around you.

Optional extensions to this reflection

1) If you are comfortable with extending this exercise, you can then see the rays of the sun shining to the center of every cell of your body and then see them shining like suns in themselves, expanding in size. Now focus on the space between each cell entering into that space until you find yourself amid the Milky Way galaxy, with every star around you being a cell within your body.

2) After you send the missiles of love to the sun and create that thread of contact, enter within the secret chamber of your heart walk into the shining white pearl, travel to the white fire core of the sun and sit before it like you would meditating in the inner recesses of your heart, keeping your inner self there as you return to your day.

Focus on the shining white pearl within your heart as being an outpost emitting the white fire core from the heart of the

149

sun onto everything around you.

The more you practice being co-present in the world, in time you'll be able to see more and remember more of your time there.

But remember... Shhhhh... it's a secret ;) The less you share with the outer world, the more these inner realms will start opening up to you.

Meditation exercise: enjoy the sunset

Take half an hour out of your evening tonight to sit in solitude watching the sunset. Try not to look at this as a burden on your evening schedule but more so a gift, for your efforts today.

A reward for you and you alone.

As you sit, take a second to briefly meditate slowing down your mind to the speed of life. Open your eyes once you feel you've broken through all sense of urgency. Observe your senses as you get to the stage of the sun descending and the sky changing to all the different golden and peachy tones.

This is an active meditation, meaning you are meditating with your eyes open.

Let us now bring our senses into the experience.

Send love through your eyes at what you can see.

What can you hear around you?

Listening gracefully, trying to pour your whole heart into those moments of silence.

Keep looking at the tones in the sky with love.

Keep listening with love to the ambient sounds you hear around you.

If you are sitting, try to touch something around you with

your fingertips filling your sense of touch with love.

Now your senses are engaged, lets compound the experience with our breath.

Breathe in deeply through your nose, imagining your breathing in the fire from the heart of the sun.

Hold it in, then breathe out, imagining your fire breath is breathing into the sun and making it intensify in heat, like when you breathe into a fire.

You can now enter into the secret chamber of your heart sitting before the shining white pearl and blue, yellow, and pink flames.

Expand the flames onto the image of the sunset blending the primary colors of the flame in your heart to make the colors tones in the sunset.

You can also now begin expanding yourself in size. Imagine the sun being drawn into your heart and becoming the size of the shining white pearl within your heart, so even when seeing the view of the sunset, the pearl within your heart is the point that is sending love and light to the world around you.

After some practice, if you semi-squint your eyes, you can choose to travel into the sun in the finer body of your inner self as well.

Enjoy the experience until the sun descends, and thank your heart and the sun for the moment.

The next time you sit and watch a sunset will be even better.

Things to consider

We have covered a lot in this previous chapter, where I have given you a lot of visualizations, which are potential meditations to work on and experiment with. If you want to write them out on the notes on your phone and try them later, you'll benefit from it. I want to keep this book very practical for even those who choose not to dig deep, hence, the reason for two active meditations.

It feels incredible to be able to do these exercises with no thoughts or feelings trying to pull you in a different direction from what you are doing. If you find them boring to start with, in time, you'll discipline yourself to make this a sacred moment for you and your inner self.

These active meditations are also recharging, so having a handful of both styles of meditating gives you the option to squeeze many moments throughout the day performing short meditations to realign yourself.

Going through the exercise of mirroring the sun after time becomes automated. You will find yourself being invigorated when you greet the sun or see the sun in the sky each day.

I hold so many personal experiences in my heart from starting to experiment with connecting with the sun more. It was almost instantly within the first week, the sun started working with me, like I had a friend working with me to achieve the same goal.

For example, I am driving to work, busy in thought, then I feel the warmth of the sun starting to bleed through the clouds, and I am brought back into alignment, filling my heart with a surge of love like the sun had given me a warm hug.

When working on mirroring the sun, it becomes unconscious, too. So when you feel the sun, you automatically align to it. It is also another dimension of something working with you to remind you to realign yourself to where you have days where this golden disc above you will complement your connection to and with everything.

In regards to the sunset meditation, you may have a period when you're doing it diligently, and then it will drop off for a while as you are pulled into the responsibilities of life. I haven't been able to stop and enjoy every sunset, but the months and years I spent practicing this have helped anchor so many memories within my heart. When you step outside at night and see the peachy sky, you are more aware of it. I often feel at times like my inner child is yanking on my hand saying, "Hey, look at this one."

I don't actually hear that being said, but it's more of the feeling of an excited child trying to bring my attention to something.

Remember the motto of our book: *Repetition equals retention.*

Our ultimate aim with this book is to make our daily life a sequence of sacred moments to hold us in that space or bring us back when we fall out of that space. This ritual of watching the sun descend for the day is one of those moments you can make a little more magical.

This chapter was indeed a deep one, but I promise you that if you invest time into building a personal relationship with the sun, you will understand the love in my words when I speak to the sun so much more.

10

The Breath of Life: Harnessing Vital Energy

In this next chapter, let us focus on breath. Did you know that on average we take around **22,000** breaths a day?

Think about that for a second...

Now, out of those **22,000** breaths, how many do you think you have been fully conscious of?

It's okay; you are not alone. This is something I am working on personally, and that's to try and be more mindful of my breath. I believe when someone gets this, they get everything, and that's because we are always breathing. Not to mention that I have seen phenomenal improvement within myself in only a short time, so if you choose to focus on this, I know you could make massive strides really quickly. If anyone puts in the effort to become more constantly conscious of their breathing, it is unquestionable that their life will change for the better.

Let us trace back to the first meditation session, where we gave three full breaths to the count of eight seconds and how invigorated we felt after running through the exercise.

Imagine how good you would feel even after 10 minutes of

breathing like this and the space it would put you in?

Now imagine how you'd feel after an hour of breathing in that way and the space it would put you in?

Without a doubt breath in itself is the most overlooked action in our daily lives.

Let me give you some examples: the Shaolin monks have demonstrated freely for hundreds of years the ability to per-form superhuman power and strength by using breathing methods invoking 'chi' before they strike something or absorb the impact of a blow to their body.

Another example would be the Eastern mystics; they, too, understood the importance of breath and breathing. Both Pranayama and Taoist breathing are two spiritual disciplines that have been around and have existed for thousands of years, where it is taught and believed that everywhere around us is this life force that can be invoked or summoned through breathing.

For anyone skeptical about what I am saying, just because our eyes can't physically see something doesn't mean it fails to exist.

We can't see radio waves or the Wi-Fi that powers our mobile phones, yet we still acknowledge their presence.

Gravity is another example: We all hold faith in this unseen force in action and believe in its existence.

Most of us can go weeks without food and days without water, but if our breath is cut off, we'll inevitably last ten minutes at the most.

I am sharing these concepts and thoughts to help you understand how important breathing is. I hope you prioritize this area of your life more.

So, what is the first thing we can do to remove the veil of

ignorance?

The easiest way is to start by being grateful, meaning to start seeing every breath we take as a gift. It is a gift. From the first breath at birth to the last breaths we take in those final moments of life.

Now, I'm not saying you must be centered and mindful for every one of the 22,000 breaths of the day you take...

At the same time, I am not saying it's impossible.

With a little focus on being more mindful of our breathing, every jewel we experience throughout the days of our lives will instantly be amplified.

Breathe with love

I have already spoken about integrating love and putting it behind the five senses; now we are going to repeat the process of putting love behind our breath.

The easiest way to start this is to imagine yourself hugging someone you love and then breathe in and out while you picture yourself hugging them.

Try one breath now for a moment...

· Take a deep breath in through your nose while feeling that fuzzy feeling of hugging someone.
· Hold your breath in now, hugging the air you're holding in your lungs.
· Picture that you are pouring love from your heart and filling the air within your lungs with love.
· Then breathe out as if you were sending love-charged air to the person you are picturing yourself hugging.

If you have no one special to think of, you could think of a pet, a hobby or something you love doing to help.

You'll only need to do this three or four times thinking about the hug to charge your breath and then you'll be able to do it without using the hug to charge the action of breathing.

Hugs are awesome, though, so you can keep using them. You can even picture that you are hugging yourself.

Random question here, but what's your favourite color?

- What if you visualized the air you were breathing in and out as being that color?
- What about if you visualized the air you are breathing in and out as being pink?
- What about if you visualized the air you breathe as being diamond-white?
- What about if you visualized the air you breathe as being gold?
- Which color is your favorite to visualize?

Pick a color and experiment while you are reading this chapter.

Please note: Just a suggestion: If your favorite color is black, brown or red, I wouldn't recommend it long term; choose something brighter.

Seeing it as white fire, tinged with golden pink is my personal favourite

Breathe from the bottom of your belly

Many years ago, my doctor taught me the correct breathing

method.

She used to say that the average person would breathe with only the top third of their lungs, which often led to anxiety as the air and energy around the solar plexus and belly region weren't moving. She then taught me the correct method of pushing out your stomach while you are breathing in until your belly pops out like you had eaten too much.

It takes some time to practice but becomes automatic after a while. Because you are pushing your stomach out while you are breathing in, you are creating a void in the lungs, which sucks the air into the bottom third of the lungs, giving you more air and strengthening the lungs to breathe in air to fill the whole lungs.

After building a habit with this, whenever you sense any tension in the belly, you can circulate the energy in that region and move it on by breathing out the tension within a breath or two.

Through my personal experience, I noticed instant results through practicing this. First, it was a powerful tool to combat anxiety in my earlier days when I used to wrestle with it more, and also, after practicing it for a while, I noticed my overall lung capacity expanded, meaning every breath was more invigorating.

- The easiest way to start building a habit like this is to begin breathing like this through your daily meditations.
- You could then add it to your hourly alarm sequence to realign yourself.
- If you do physical activity and ever find yourself short of breath, try pushing out your belly to breathe in.
- Anytime you feel any emotion within yourself that you

don't want, you can use this exercise to move it on too.

Pause the book for a second now and try it for yourself.

Breathing in through your nose

This is a no brainer right?

So why would I need to share this?

That's because hardly anyone does it. Or at least does it consistently enough to see the real benefit in it?

Just as breathing from the belly helps to clear our emotions, breathing through the nose helps to clear our minds. Then, when you also add the extra dimension of visualizing color or sunlight within the air you breathe, it makes it even more powerful again.

I found the best way to self-correct yourself is to touch the roof of your mouth with the tip of your tongue. Now, hold it there. Try breathing through your mouth now; I bet you can't.

Why not try holding your tongue on the roof of your mouth while you're typing away at the computer or the next time you drive your car?

This is the easiest way to get the ball rolling and start building a new habit.

Once you have built a momentum of breathing through your nose, I find it really helpful to start tracing the breath as it enters your nose, up through the front of your forehead, to the top of your skull, then down the back of your skull and down your spine into your belly or stomach.

Breathe to fan the flame of your heart

When you are holding a flat piece of cardboard and fanning a fire, the coals light up and glow intensely, and the flames grow larger. You see the fire thriving stronger as the extra air blowing onto the flames fuels it. I want you to see the same thing happening when we breathe in and out, as if our breath is fanning the flame within our hearts.

Regardless, if you have felt the love I have been speaking of or just a sense of harmony and comfort, that feeling within your heart can still be kindled and nurtured.

When looking at a picture of the anatomy of the organs, you can see how both the lungs surround the heart, almost like the heart is a campfire within a cave. Even without using this visualization, you can see the air travelling through the lungs inevitably nurtures the heart.

Breaths then start becoming breaths of joy as we begin breathing to fan the heart's flame. It is the flame of the heart that invigorates our being. Then, from moment to moment, everyday experiences around us start becoming ever more special.

Breathing to anchor yourself

Feeling a little lightheaded or like you're being pushed around by the events happening around you?

This quick reset is awesome and works.

Stop for a second and stand with both feet flat on the ground, slightly pushing your heels down into the ground, then imagine a string on the top of your head gently pulling you up, opening up your spine and making you stand more tall and straight.

Now take a big, long and slow breath in through your nose,

tracing it all the way from your head down your spine to fill your stomach; hold it in for a moment, then let it out.

Pause for a second.

Focus on that open emptiness you feel while pausing. The feeling is similar to the feeling felt when we were giving the earlier exercises in listening gracefully.

Hold your attention on that feeling, continuing with your day. Your emotions and feelings should start mirroring the feeling of emptiness.

Breathe in your moments with nature

Those little moments where you are moved by nature, whether it's an intentional exercise to compound your senses into the moment or it's just something you notice quickly on your travels, practice breathing in the moment, like you are breathing in everything you can see in through your nose, and hold it in and love it. When you breathe out, breathe out with love sending that moment back to the area you took it from.

If you try this four or five times, watch how the joy starts to build in your heart and starts snowballing with anticipation, awaiting the next moment around the corner that will move you.

Expand the area you are breathing from

Have you ever tried to expand the area of where you are breathing from?

It's fun to play around with the idea that we are bigger than this big clump of flesh we live in and call our bodies.

Try this: place your attention on the edges of the perimeter and fence line of the property or location you are in. If you have to go outside to do this, do it. Now try breathing in and imagine the air is coming from each corner of the property.

Now, let the air out, sending it back out to each corner of the property.

Now take another 10 breaths in the same way to stretch your limitations in breathing.

The more you practice and get comfortable with this, the more you can then start stretching it even further, like to the edges and every corner of your city, or even your country or as far as you can stretch your awareness.

Breathing to surrender

This next gem here is so good once you get the knack of it.

We've touched lightly on surrendering before; this will add another level to it and is one I've had excellent results with.

Looking at any challenging situation you face before even taking it on, stop, pause, and breathe in the problem. Hold it in your heart, love it, surrender it, and then let it go. Just like you were letting go of a helium balloon, the moment you open your hands and let go of the string, you watch it rise and float away from you.

Now, you are completely detached from it because you did this when you took on the problem. When I say detached, I mean it's a little harder for you to overreact or get stressed as you've completely surrendered to love to help resolve the issue. Try it a couple of times and see if it works for you. It's more adding breathing into the ritual of surrendering, which is the stepping stone to using your breath as a tool to help you. In this instance, you're using your breath to catch the problem, then breathing out after you surrender to the issue to help you break any personal block within yourself preventing you from resolving the issue. These blocks often lodge themselves within us when we face challenges like this. You can also experiment with using your breath to help resolve problems around you by breathing in and seeing your breathing in the problem or people around you, then holding in your breath and loving it. Then see when you breathe out, your love has transmuted the problem and your letting it go and rise up like steam.

You can also try breathing out onto a problem you see around you or something that you are facing seeing your breath as a pink-white fire transmuting the problem if you want to get a little more creative.

"Who do you think you are, a love dragon?"

Laugh all you want, I do this all the time and watch anger between people move, situations resolve them self, and others step in to help me. Don't move your lips or make it look obvious like you're breathing on people. Just do it subtly and softly; it's more like you're sending the flame of your heart through your breath onto an issue. This is an advanced tip, try it for yourself once you have a lot more consistency with all the other points in this book.

Breathing to raise up others

This part here is for the champions to read. Those who want to bring up the whole world around them. You've been doing all this breathwork and see massive changes within yourselves now when others are around you, maybe processing or venting their emotions about a problem. Why not try breathing in their pain, like you're trying to take it off their shoulders?

We've transmuted so many personal blocks and baggage through our journey so far; it gets so much easier to transmute the baggage in the world that's outside of yourself.

Breathe it in, hold in your breath and transmute the issue with love. Then, as you breathe out, see the problem within the air you're breathing out as being similar to helium floating up above you rather than returning to the person you are helping who you took it from.

Or maybe you see people arguing, and as well as seeing those golden-purple ripples of peace floating from your solar plexus towards them to dissipate the problem, you choose to also breathe out a long and slow breath of love into the issue to help melt all the anger and hardness of heart they are currently feeling.

The more you begin co-creating with love, the more your heart will be filled with love to where you'll be able to fill a room with love if you choose, and in time the area even the size of a football field or city.

Absorb everything I say and then choose what's right for you

I've built this book to help anyone at any level of life. You may not be drawn as much into the spiritual areas of the book, but more into the practical ones. Awesome, I know you've definitely got enough tools to work on.

For myself, I found through clearing my thoughts and feelings and meditating while living mindfully; these spiritual dimensions started opening for me naturally; my guess is that this may happen for others, but then again, maybe it won't.

Let's say you choose to leave the spiritual parts of the book to the side for now, and in two or three years, something happens that drives you to start pursuing this area in life, we often go through different cycles in life. That's when you know that it's time to pick this book up again and that there is more work to do.

Breathing from the shining white pearl

Once you incorporate all these other skills into your breathing, the next level of breathing is to start breathing from the shining white pearl within your heart. You are welcome to start focusing on this immediately, or you can incorporate the other tips into your life and then work towards integrating this as your next step towards mastery of breath. This is your choice.

In earlier chapters, I spoke of fanning the fire within the shining white pearl as an exercise to help center yourself. Essentially, this tip here is a continuation of this, but more so, as you build your connection and awareness to this inner self within that secret chamber within your heart, you become more aware of being out in the world but still present within your heart. You breathe in, drawing in the fire and energy from the shining white pearl within your heart, and then, as you breathe back into the pearl, this fire within you builds in intensity.

This fire can then become an internal fire, spreading all through your body, or even become a flame outside of yourself, looking like an invisible white fire tinged with golden pink, surrounding you, nine feet in diameter, then eventually bigger the more you practice breathing with it.

In the previous chapter, I touched briefly on visualizing your favourite spot in the world you've been to and travelling there in the heart through entering the shining white pearl. You can think of that, or you can see those higher etheric levels of formlessness reached through our meditations. If you start breathing from the same place you've been travelling to, you will inevitably fill your body with a similar vibration.

Even if you imagine the shining white pearl as a balloon filled with air and you breathe it in to start with and breathe out to fill it again, practicing this will help add another dimension to your life.

I hope this is clear and makes sense.

If you build a habit with this, you are no longer just breathing oxygen to sustain your body; you're fueling it with something else.

Reflection exercise: charge your cells with breath

This exercise can be done while sitting or lying down, whichever you prefer.

Firstly, close your eyes, centering yourself, and bring all the energies of your thoughts and feelings into the center of your heart.

Focused completely on your heart, you see your heart light up like a sphere of white light.

Shining brightly, see it shining like the sun lighting up our solar system.

Let each breath you breathe in intensify the light of your heart.

Let each breath you breathe out also intensify the light of your heart.

Now, visualize little replicas of your heart within every cell in your body shining brightly with the same light as your heart.

Let the light rays spread all through your body as points of brilliant white light.

Wiggle your toes and see the white points fill your toes.

Then wiggle your fingers and see the pinpoints of light shining brightly within your hands and fingers, your arms and legs, now see them all at once through every bit of your body.

See every cell of your body is a pinpoint of the same white light.

Now breathe through your nose, intensifying the light within the center of every cell in your body, then breathe out through your mouth, fanning and intensifying the light within every cell of your body.

When you feel the time is right, slowly open your eyes.

With your eyes open, keep breathing in and out, seeing and feeling your breath as fanning the shining white light within every cell of your being.

Try to continue seeing your breath intensify the light in the cells of your being for thirty more minutes if you want a challenge.

You can do it; keep focusing on your breathing.

You can then journal your thoughts or experiences, if you choose.

Tip: *Set an alarm on your phone for thirty minutes if you are serious about trying*

Meditation exercise: the sacred breath of life

For this meditation, let us get comfortable and close our eyes.

This meditation is to assist us with building a subconscious momentum of breathing mindfully on a larger scale and area.

Center yourself and breathe in through your nose while pushing out your diaphragm so your lungs fully fill with air.

Now, exhale through your mouth, seeing the air you breathe as being a white fire tinged with golden pink. See this golden-pink-tinged white fire travelling out in every direction from you and throughout the world.

In that moment in between your breath, you have already stretched your awareness to every point on the planet.

Now breathe back in through your nose, seeing that breath of fire returning to you tenfold and fanning the flame of your heart and filling every cell of your body with even more love.

With the added momentum, you breathe out again, seeing the same golden-pink-tinged white fire breathe in all directions, encompassing the whole planet.

Feeling the love you have sent out in all directions, it comes back as you breathe in through your nose, multiplied even more, fanning the flame of your heart and every cell of your body.

With even more momentum, breathe out and bless the world, seeing the flame of your heart in the center of the earth, with your golden-pink-tinged white fire breath encompassing the earth again.

This time feel every person on the planet, as if the fire in your breath has lit a candle within their hearts.

Now, as you breathe in, see your breath returning to you tenfold, with every heart on the planet being drawn into you with your breath.

Your heart has increased in size; it is now bigger than the planet itself.

Hold everyone in your heart all at once as you breathe out and bless the earth again.

Let each breath from here on make the flames of everyone's candles burn brighter and brighter.

Try to give thirty more breaths like this before you conclude this meditation.

When you open your eyes, reflect on how you feel.

Imagine if you were breathing like this **22,000** times a day?

You may wish to journal your experiences after completing this exercise.

Things to consider

With the reflection exercise, after I ask you to open your eyes and continue seeing your cells, this meditation then becomes an active meditation. Having your breaths lighten up every cell of your body. After giving this once or twice, you can try giving it throughout the day if you feel prompted to intensify any moment you are in, if you choose.

You can also experiment with turning up the light within your heart and cells with that imaginary dimmer switch we've been using in previous exercises to shine the cells in your being brighter on command once you have practiced this for a while and feel confident.

Tracing every cell in your body can be difficult the first couple of times, but the brain works the same way as drawing a mind map on paper, drawing neurons outside the original neuron and linking them; once you do it and succeed in projecting your consciousness outside of your skull it is easier to do in future once you've stretched yourself and mapped light filling your cells of your body once.

With the breathing meditation, your effort will put you in the greatest space, so get a little excited about practicing this.

Every moment you spend meditating on your breaths being sent throughout the whole planet makes it easier to summon more energy from your breaths through your daily life to where you feel the breath is coming not just into your mouth and nose, but you are drawing it from the entire planet. We want to build an unconscious habit to where we are always breathing on a planetary scale.

Well, that is what I am aiming for ;)

You can also try experimenting with breathing in the pains and burdens of the world once you connect with the hearts of those around the world, consuming them with the fire of your heart, and sending love back to fill the void from where the burdens were originally taken.

Then, you can think of breathing into specific locations if you choose to experiment more. The same exercise, but more targeted.

I am still experimenting with using the breath more creatively; having an always-learning attitude is what makes life so much more fun.

11

True Power: Tapping Into Your Inner Strength

Now that we are well on the way to operating more effectively with love, it is time for us to touch lightly on power and how we can govern it more correctly. The more we start governing power correctly, the more power will be given to us.

So many people in the world are chasing power, focusing purely on gaining power but failing to cultivate love.

People who fail to lead with love often are more critical and blunt with their words and can become tyrannical.

Fortunately for us, though, we have already been exploring love and are beginning to fan the flame of love in our lives. If we continue working on this, it will help us with balancing the power we send out daily.

Power follows love effortlessly, yet, there are a few laws we need to understand first in order to ensure we are governing power correctly.

Once understood and practiced correctly, life becomes so much more enjoyable as we find ourselves with more energy and more creativity, and our tasks and projects are completed much more easily.

What do I mean by power?

When I speak about power, I am talking about the energy we are putting into motion to complete our tasks and projects.

Think of electrical power and how that works for a moment. Once you flick the main switch to send electricity to a house, electricity flows through and operates in every area of the house. Let us use this as a visual to help us see a blue electricity flowing through us and into everything we say and do.

Power is sent through our speech and actions as we are active in our days. There are many, many varieties of power in action throughout the world. I want us to focus on the power being distributed through our four lower bodies and optimize this area within ourselves: physical power, emotional power, mental power, and spiritual power. Spiritual power flows through our memory or etheric body, which can also be seen as coming from the shining white pearl and blue plume of flame above it.

When you see people that are super productive and manage to get a lot of things done, quite often, its because they are using their power correctly and flowing with power.

This is the ultimate goal for everyone of us to make maximum use of the time while we are here. My goal for you is to help you with mastering this area in your life, that is, if you haven't already, so listen closely.

Re-read this chapter repeatedly if this is an area of your life you need to work on. The first step is to focus on conserving power, as by conserving power from having our energy stolen from the things that are stealing our daily energy, we will have so much more energy to put into the things we want to see done.

Power is given to us daily

Every morning that we wake in the morning a daily increment of power is given to us. Think of it like a gallon of fuel we have to invest into our day.

Where we choose to direct this energy in the morning will usually determine whether we feel charged by the afternoon, or feel low in energy and flat. This chapter is super important; so if you think I am steering away from the topic of mindfulness, I assure you I am not.

I am trying to teach you its wrong to feed your monkey mind a banana for breakfast by grabbing your smartphone as soon as you wake up!

Our first moments in the morning are sacred, remember that. Let's work towards framing a perfect day.

If we can control our mornings, we have more hope in controlling our days.

If we use this first surge of energy in the morning on ourselves, nurturing our connection with our inner self, we start the day on a win.

That could be giving a short morning meditation, a light workout, a 25-minute block of deep, focused work or studying towards one of our personal projects, or even trying to build a sequential ritual where you are able to incorporate all three.

Once completing those first tasks, how good would it be to spend five or ten minutes completely present and undistracted with your children, family, or partner and fill their hearts with love and excitement to take with them to start their day?

If you live by yourself, even better, let's focus on you. Try to turn making your morning smoothie or breakfast into a ritual of love. Once you've had your breakfast, (or coffee, if you're intermittent fasting), after you've done those things, then, you can grab your phone. It only takes you 10 minutes, tops, to scroll through your emails and your messages. However, just by completing your morning ritual first thing before touching your phone, you've started your day on a win. When you leave the house for work, you've framed the day, so even if it went pear-shaped from here, you'd still wake up tomorrow one step closer to your ultimate goal.

Do this for four or five days straight and watch how much more energy you start running with throughout the day, it's awesome.

The alternative to this is waking up, grabbing your phone, scrolling through your messages, Facebook, and emails, and using the blue light as your morning coffee to wake yourself up, then scroll through your news feed, reels, and shorts, like you're playing the slot machines trying to win a hit of dopamine. Then, pull yourself out of the matrix and roll out of bed feeling flat, pushing yourself to get in the shower to get your day started.

This doesn't sound like anyone you know, does it?

What we don't realise, though, is that receiving emails and messages and looking at posts on social media throws your mind in so many different directions that you've stuffed your day before its even started. Our minds aren't built to operate like this, especially first thing in the morning. So you've rattled your mind to where it will be darting and bouncing around the room and off the walls like one of those little bouncy balls you used to get when you were kids.

'How To Be More Mindless and Procrastinate.'

Not a book I want to read anymore.

That fuel you had to start your day on a win, has now been syphoned and leaked out to all those things you were looking at on social media and your creative surge for the day has now been stolen from you. When you respond to those emails and messages, your creative fuel has gone out into the world to the receiver and not you.

Now you are wondering why it's not even 11:30 am at work and you are struggling and feeling flat at work today and already on your third coffee?

This is why we need to minimize the outer distractions in the morning and focus on ourselves first. Getting those most important tasks out of the way is key.

Try this for three or four days straight if you don't believe me and see where life starts taking you.

You'll have so much more pep in your step.

I suggest jotting down on paper or in your phone's notes three or four things you could do every morning to really own the day. Then, experiment with starting your day fully focused on completing those three or four things and getting them done before turning your phone on or switching it from aeroplane mode.

Then, from there, start trying to hit your target. You may not get it all in to start with, but it will start giving you something to strive for to better yourself.

Watch how your confidence and energy levels start to boom and soar after practicing this as well.

The power of your focus

The law of attraction or the law of attention states that whatever we focus on is what we'll bring into our lives. Meaning that if we concentrate on chaos and negativity, we will attract more negative things to us because our attention is manifesting them.

Ever wondered why life has been so unjust at times?

Change your focus.

Many people talk about the benefits of keeping a gratitude journal, as by focusing on things to be grateful for, they don't waste energy on negative thoughts. Focusing on the positive things in your world and aligning with positive energy attracts more positive experiences, people, and opportunities into their lives.

In short, like attracts like. So, if you are having one of those negative days where everything seems like a struggle, switch it up.

Focus on four or five good things that are going on in your world right now.

Lock onto the good things in your world and love them while you focus on addressing any problem you are facing. Watch how quickly the issues you are facing start fading away, and you turn your day around.

The power in faith

I've touched on faith briefly already. Faith is a power in itself, as by holding faith in any situation we are bringing constant power into action.

If you can practice holding faith on issues within your heart when needed, you'll smash through any initiation or test you're facing.

It hurts me to see faith as being labelled as a religious thing and not for life itself, which is limiting so many in the world from practicing to using this power.

It's this easy. Whatever test you're facing or problem you're trying to fix, what's your desired outcome?

What do you want to see happen?

Cast your imagination into the future and visualize the scene of what you want to happen, then hold that vision in your heart and wrap it in love.

This is faith.

Using this tool when life sends us chaos helps us to grab the wheel of life and steer us back on track.

Let's run through a couple more examples: think of the time you have spent meditating and how good it felt once your thoughts and feelings settled and you started entering into that space between your thoughts... You started to feel recharged from being in that space of emptiness.

You can almost enter into it again just by thinking about it.

Now think about a moment when you've been wound up in your thoughts or your emotions almost paralysing you, caus-ing you to be overwhelmed by everything that's happening.

You already know you can settle your thoughts and feelings and they will settle.

You know what it feels like when you settle and start to enter what I call the 'cloud-like consciousness', meaning you're floating comfortably, just enjoying watching the world around you.

Now, because you know you're thoughts and feelings will settle and you can remember, see, and feel what it feels like from previous meditations, you steer yourself back into alignment.

This is faith.

This also shows us an example of using the power of focus correctly, but I have used it in the example of faith, as it illustrates how by holding faith in our hearts of what we already know is about to happen, we can set the power of faith in motion.

Another example could be you make a mistake at work or break something. It's one of those days. Everything just seems to be going wrong no matter how much you try to fix it all. You catch yourself, stop, and surrender to all the chaos around you and face yourself. You know this chaos won't last forever, so you realign your emotional energies to start flowing with love again and march on to face the problem. With faith in your heart, you plough through and break through every block until the issues are resolved.

This is faith.

When it's raining, the sun is still shining behind the clouds, isn't it?

The sun is always shining, just like our hearts are always shining and everything around us we are starting to connect with more. We must hold faith and know that every situation will correct itself and that feeling of comfort will return. If you hold faith, knowing that the state of harmony will restore itself, the power in faith will manifest it.

Once you practice this, you become unshakable.

You become like this rock, anchored so firmly in faith that no matter how strong the waves of life are crashing down from around you, nothing can move you or steal your energy.

Even if we cannot be in alignment 100% of the time, we can use faith to help us close those gaps in between and choose which reality we'd rather experience.

The power within our heart

For those who have been enjoying the meditation on the secret chamber of the heart, you can start seeing the brilliant electric blue plume of flame as being power in its purest form. Ponder on this next time you see this flame pulsing and dancing to the rhythm of your heartbeat while meditating.

Meditating on this blue plume out of the three flames pulsing within your heart will help you bring more balanced power into your life in all you do.

If you want to start becoming creative with it, you can begin experimenting with centering yourself and visualizing that three-colored flame within your heart and focusing on the blue flame before you speak, complete tasks, or while leading others.

The power in congruency

Have you ever been at a bar and felt an unusual urge to have a drink?

Or maybe you've been out shopping, and even though you're usually frugal with money, you find yourself getting carried away with buying something random?

There are pools of accumulated energy from other people's habits and momentums that we often can't sense or see, but quite often, we can unknowingly be pulled into them if our guard isn't up.

Let us look at this as happening on a planetary scale as well.

For instance, if you get angry at someone or something, you begin tuning into the planetary momentum of anger. The same goes for any negative emotions like fear or anxiety. Think about the exercise we went through in an earlier chapter using a radio station dial to tune through different emotions, and then we tuned into the channel of anger.

There are a lot of people broadcasting the same channel as you, which can explain why people sometimes get really angry or really scared for no reason.

Makes you realise why it is a lot harder to much those habits we want to change and why it can often be hard to settle our thoughts and feelings once we start trying to walk the higher path to life.

There is a good side to this too, as this also goes for positive thoughts and feelings as well.

So, once we settle our feelings and enter a feeling of peace and harmony, we are then held and supported by everyone else who is emanating that vibration from themselves to the planet.

Once you enter into a feeling of peace, be sure to ponder on this for a second and stretch your vision to think of everyone else on the planet also emanating the feeling of peace.

You have this army of hearts working with you and helping you. They want you to master this area of your life; remember that.

Whatever emotion or desire you are feeling, you are broadcasting and aligning yourself with everyone on the planet on the same vibration.

What does this mean to you?

Haha! I'm glad you asked.

Next time you align yourself to the feeling of love, joy, gratitude, peace, or any positive feeling, try this. Stop for a second and acknowledge everyone feeling the same feeling as you at that moment, and send them missiles or waves of love for a moment.

Observe the feeling that comes back to you.

You have an alliance working with you now. An alliance that is on your side and wants you to succeed in this.

Just by acknowledging this power in congruency and everyone else on the planet sending the same positive emotions as you, you have entered into this antakaranah with some of the highest souls evolving on the planet. Not to mention that their momentum on this vibration will help hold you up as well if you find yourself slipping into negative emotions often.

If you can feel this congruency I speak of and that added level of love you've aligned yourself to, then congratulations, you've just made it to base camp, which is the first camp spot for those climbing Mount Everest, the highest mountain on the planet. Celebrate the victory for a moment, then take my hand, and let's keep going, for we have so much more to go.

Race you to the top!!

The power in the word

The more we hold our harmony, the more we see what happens to the world around us when we speak. If we are heart-centered when we deliver our words, we share the attainment of our heart into the world around us. Our words can serve to lift life up, but at the same time, we can also tear down the world around us with our words as well.

Criticizing, condemning, judging others, or engaging in gossip is an utter no-no.

This goes for condemning ourselves as well and critisizing ourselves on our actions. Never, ever put yourself down, the second you do, you put yourself outside that circle of oneness and start filling yourself with negativity, doubt, and low confidence.

Now, you may have friends or family members who engage in gossip and speak critically of others; this is quite common.

- *So... How can we start to correct this?*

To start with, monitor yourself when you see it happening or you catch yourself engaging with it.

There is a temporary good feeling felt when speaking critically of others. It's not real, though, it's kind of like drinking alcohol to feel happy; it's an artificial buzz.

It's going to be harder for you from here, as I'm bringing things to your attention now you won't be able to unsee.

If you want to look at starting to self-correct yourself, this is the first thing you can do. Assess yourself and the type of person you want to be by asking these two questions:

- *What if they were in the room?*
- *Would you say the same thing as you are saying now?*

Now, imagine what the person you're speaking critically with says about you when you're not around. Regardless of whether that person is loyal to you or not, this quick reflection helps position yourself as the one receiving the criticism or gossip to help you empathize with the person being torn down by words when they are not around. I say it like that because, bluntly, that is what it is.

It can get tough having to self-reflect and look at the things we are doing wrong, but we must go through the uncomfortable to get more comfortable. The first step is becoming aware of what we are doing and then having the desire and drive to work towards fixing it.

I don't care what you did yesterday; today is all that matters, so I expect you to be the same.

This helps you see we are putting power into action when we speak, and if we correct this area and only speak to raise life because we are not perverting our power, it will begin to build and snowball. I challenge you to prove me wrong.

Remember, we are working towards becoming that better person we visualized in the first reflection. Everyone who reads these words gets to choose for themselves how far they run with what I am saying.

I'll leave you with a quote to ponder on now and whenever you're facing this topic in the future.

"I often regret that I have spoken, never that I have been silent." - Publilius Syrus.

It's a quote I have made my own. I ask you to make it yours as well.

Stop swearing and cursing

Try to stop swearing or cursing. Swearing is used to vent anger or react to something with frustration, whereas cursing is when you use swear words to hurt or label others.

Here are some reasons why you shouldn't swear:
your aligning your emotions to the feelings of anger.
You're misusing your power of speech.
With the law of congruency, you've just aligned yourself to everyone else swearing on the planet.

If we can drop all the glamour pushed on us as teenagers that it is cool to swear, it does nothing but lower our character and how we're perceived by others.

It's the lowest level of communication, devolving you to the level of a caveman or cavewoman. "Ugh!"

The reason you shouldn't curse others swearing at them and labelling them, is because that is exactly what you are doing; cursing them. Not to the extent of a witch out of The Wizard of Oz, but the power in your words has a massive impact on the person you are swearing at.

Let me explain why: Masaru Emoto, was a renowned author and pseudoscientist. In his book entitled 'The Hidden Messages in Water,' he showed photos taken of water magnified under a microscope after saying different words to the water being photographed. In photos where he said "thank you" and "I love you", the water molecule moulded into a shape similar to a snowflake, whereas, when he said the words "you fool" and "I hate you", the water molecules exploded to look like a whirlpool and perverted.

Look him up for yourself online and have a look at the images; they are fascinating.

These words are pretty soft compared to modern-day swear words, too. When you think that our bodies consist of over 60% water, and what damage you are doing by swearing and cursing others and the effect your words are actually having on them.

As you are raising yourself to become more heart-centered, it doesn't feel appropriate to swear. You also start seeing how much your energies drop when you do. If you haven't experienced this personally yet, you will start seeing it soon.

Becoming more heart-centered is the first step to correcting this habit.

Another step we can take is pausing for a couple of seconds before we speak.

Are you counting to three?

I just asked you a question??

Are you counting to three before you open your mouth?

I spoke about this before, but as soon as you start practicing the three-second pause before speaking, even if it's just during the first 30 minutes when you get to work to start with, you'll start seeing a massive improvement in yourself. Life will change very quickly for you if you do this.

When we respond to people mindlessly, it often drops us down to their level, and we put them before ourselves and ignore everything that we have been trying to weave into our worlds.

Whereas, if you pause for three seconds, your self-correction turns you to your heart, and you respond from the level of the heart, bringing more light into the situation.

Again, this is a little advanced for when you are carrying a lot more attainment, where you'll start to notice when responding to others below the level of the heart, you'll start to see staying centered and guarding the light you are holding is essential.

Was it kind? Was it necessary? Was it true?

I have three questions that will change your world if you use them and make them yours. Is it kind? Is it necessary? Is it true?

Is it kind? - Meaning, will it hurt the feelings of who you are speaking to or who you are speaking about?

Is it necessary? - Is it necessary for you to say this?

What are you putting your power into by speaking and sharing this in the world?

Do I really need to share these words with this person?

Is it true? - Is what you are about to say honest?

Are you twisting the truth in any way?

Even if you think you are doing it to serve a greater purpose?

For those choosing to take the higher path in self-correction, let us remember these three simple questions and ask ourselves them before whatever it is we are about to say.

Is it kind? Is it necessary? Is it true?

If it makes it past these three filters, it is usually safe to voice what we want to say.

Idle chatter

Be mindful of idle chatter; this will drain your energy and power so fast, believe me. While you feel that temporary high while being in the moment gas bagging after the conversation closes and you are forced to face yourself again, you'll often notice a difference in your energy levels.

Furthermore, understand we are all creatures of free will and that you'll need to find your own balance in your life and what works for you.

When you think of the people at work or on the phone you often have a long and unnecessary conversation with, sometimes keeping it brief can serve you well.

This allows you to use the energy you have saved by not talking to keep moving forward and take on the tasks that need completing to finish the day with a victory.

Reflective exercise: grounding ourselves

Grounding meditations and exercises are a big thing. If you search online you will find a lot of content on various styles of grounding. I am going to share a grounding exercise I personally use myself that, once understood and practiced; you can give it all day if you choose.

Grounding really helps when you are feeling light-headed and wound up in the mind. This is common for people who think and are over processing everything a lot in their heads. However, a lot of the time, it's just your physical body trying to tell you it's hungry. Try eating something solid next time you feel spacey or light-headed and see if that helps as well.

For the exercise, though, let us go outside, somewhere with grass or dirt is preferred so that you can connect to the earth. However, it can be done on the carpet or any surface if that's not possible. I want you to take off your shoes and stand up.

Close your eyes once you are standing comfortably and start rocking slowly from side to side, stepping gently off the ground below you as you rock each side.

Try to notice the feeling or sensation you get when your feet make contact with the ground.

Try to slow it down where it is even softer as your foot touches the ground, making more gradual contact with the ground and slowly easing to rest your body weight on each foot as it steps on the ground.

Keep rocking and stepping on each foot.

Now try to slow down the steps to half the speed and make it even slower.

Imagine you're stepping in a puddle of water and trying not to cause any ripples gracefully.

As we step, imagine love seeping from your heart down your leg and through your feet into the ground.

Stop for a second from stepping, and imagine yourself hugging the earth with your feet as you touch the ground.

Imagine the earth now sending you love or hugging you back.

Eyes still closed, let us take a second to absorb the moment.

Now, I want you to open your eyes and repeat the exercise:

- Rocking left and right.
- Stepping slowly and gracefully.
- Establishing a connection with the earth.
- Stopping for a second to love through your feet to the ground below you.

Let's try walking forward now, and turning the rocking into steps, still stepping slowly and gracefully, sending love through our feet into the ground.

Whether you're walking up and down the area or just taking random steps, it doesn't matter.

We are trying to turn this rocking exercise into our basic steps now.

I want you to pick up the tempo now as if you are walking at half the speed you usually would.

It may take some time, but if you can add this extra layer of mindfulness into your everyday steps, another level of joy will be added into your life.

If you are constant and keep sending love into the earth as you are stepping, you should find, in time, the ground will start loving you back.

A lot of people dump their weight when they step on their feet and stand on the spot.

Play around by stepping gracefully and distributing your weight gently, as if you were trying not to make a noise at night and wake anyone up, or as I said before, walking through puddles of water without making any ripples. The care you are putting into stepping quietly will add another level of connection to what you are doing: walking gracefully.

Meditation exercise: speak from within

For this exercise, let us get comfortable and ask ourselves the questions aloud: is it kind? Is it necessary? Is it true?

Go on, stop and center yourself and say the three questions out aloud.

- Is it kind?
- Is it necessary?
- And Is it true?

Let us empty our minds and let our feelings settle, drawing our attention to the shining white pearl within our hearts.

Breathe in the white fire from the shining white pearl, and hold in the breath, letting it fill and rejuvenate every cell of your body.

Then, Breathe out onto the pearl, watching it fan and expand the blue, yellow, and pink flames above it.

Guide your four lower bodies to enter into the shining white pearl so there is no part of you outside this sacred room within your heart.

- First, your memory body
- Then your mental body
- Then, your emotional body
- And lastly, your physical body

You hear nothing but the sound of your breath, breathing in the white fire from the shining white pearl, holding in the fire within your lungs with love and embracing it as it charges and rejuvenates every cell of your being, then breathing out onto the pearl to intensify the blue, yellow, and pink plumes of flame above it.

The room lights up with the three colors of blue, yellow, and pink as you breathe on the flame, intensifying the flame as each of the three plumes increases in size to the air from your breath.

Now focus on the blue in the flame above the pearl.

It is pure power in its truest form. Breathe it in and align yourself to it, seeing yourself as being able to create with and control it.

Now you've aligned yourself to this flame of power, speak from it.

Say the words, "Is it kind? Is it necessary? Is it true?"

Say it again, from the white fire core of the pearl beneath the blue plume of fire, seeing the white fire from the pearl lighting up and expanding the blue flame above it as you say the words, "Is it kind? Is it necessary? Is it true?"

Look into the pearl now and enter into it, seeing it expand and surround you.

You travel up into higher levels of consciousness and enter what appears to be an etheric plane of formlessness existing above you in higher levels of consciousness. The scenery around you is perfect. As you gaze at perfection, it reinforces perfection onto you. From the distant waterfall, to the mountain ranges in the background that look similar appearance to the mountains in Kashmir. There is a slight tinge of blue to everything around you like it is a place of pure power. You feel it and align yourself with it.

From this place, you stand, saying the same words again, "Is it kind? Is it necessary? Is it true?"

Take a second now to connect with every element of nature around you for as long as you can see and repeat the words again, "Is it kind? Is it necessary? Is it true?"

Now say the words again, from this space, as if you are speaking from this higher plane, into the white core of the shining white pearl within your heart, and speaking through the blue flame and sending it out into the world around you below, "Is it kind? Is it necessary? Is it true?"

You are still within this higher etheric plane of consciousness.

Congratulations, my friend, you have found your inner self.

This is your inner self.

"I hope you like my book." my inner self says to your inner self.

You can come to this place whenever you choose now in meditation.

Whether you want to follow the path in front of you and see nothing but pure perfection in the scenery around you or pick the right spot to sit down and meditate is up to you.

Maybe there are more levels of these higher planes to explore?

When you are ready to end the meditation, open your eyes and return to still seeing your inner self on those inner, higher planes of consciousness.

Recite the words again from that level into the physical, "Is it kind? Is it necessary? Is it true?"

This is our goal. If we can speak and create from these higher levels, all we'll be creating and bringing into the world will be perfection.

Don't try too hard to speak from that place where your inner self is, just listen from that level. If something needs to be said, it will say it. Try to constantly surrender to it and let it lead you.

Things to consider

The reflection exercise on grounding yourself is the perfect tool to help incorporate into your daily life with stepping and standing.

It will put more pep into your step once you start walking with it.

By being cautious not to dump your body weight on the ground as you step, you are simultaneously transferring love into the ground you are stepping on.

Remember, you are stepping through puddles, trying not to make any ripples. If you merge your every day walking around to step and stand like this, watch how much more joy you'll start bringing into this world.

Once you have merged this exercise into your walking, the next step from here is to see a white fire burning up from the ground below you as you make contact with the ground with your step.

You're not visually projecting the image of white fire around you, but more knowing and feeling it blazing with your steps.

The more you practice this, the more you may experience moments where you actually see it around you.

You can also experiment with seeing the white fire blend in to have an amethyst-tinged violet tone and even merge to become completely an amethyst-violet fire at times and rotate from violet to white fire.

This is something you may not do and focus on all the time, but if you're walking somewhere in your own company, it's a fun exercise to fall back on and makes your moments with nature so much more special.

After time focusing on this, you could be standing stationary somewhere as well and experiment with seeing the fire start from the ground beneath you without stepping.

Experiment with it for yourself and see if you like it.

We can see physical fire burns and transmutes things within the physical. I am certain using this fire visualization would be able to help you in a similar way.

There are a lot of things going on in this meditation that I need to elaborate on. The first is the added dimension of entering within and using your breath to charge the cells of your being and blowing onto the pearl to balance and increase the blue, yellow, and pink flames above it. Start adding this to the start of your meditations at night and in your sequence of reconnecting when your phone sounds its alarm to reconnect throughout the day. You are still using your daily alarms aren't you?

You can also add guiding the four lower bodies into the shining white pearl afterwards, as that will help you completely surrender your outer self more.

As we start focusing on the blue power within the flame in our hearts and speaking the mantra with that blue power, then from the white fire, we are practicing speaking from the nexus of our being to transfer that spiritual power more through our words.

As we enter in the shining white pearl and travel to the higher levels of consciousness into the etheric, regardless of whether you see it clearly or not, try to feel the space you are in and practice speaking from there from the level of your inner self.

My goal of this meditation was to introduce you to the concept of having the words we speak come from the spiritual faculties of our being rather than being led by our mind. Nonetheless, this meditation has also introduced you to entering into higher levels of consciousness and a deeper understanding of your inner self. You can repeat this meditation as often as you like if you like it and mix it up, experimenting with different mantras as well. My suggestion is that you begin with some I AM affirmations, which have been scientifically proven to change people's lives for those who use them.

Pick any virtue that you are trying to embody and become a practitioner experimenting with it.

Here are a couple of suggestions to get you started:

- *"I AM free from fear and doubt."*
- *"I AM always present and connected."*
- *"I AM feeling nothing but love."*
- *"I AM forgiving all life."*
- *"I AM all life forgiving me."*
- *"I AM the balancing breath."*
- *"I AM love, wisdom, and power in perfect balance."*

Please note: the I AM Affirmation *"I AM free from fear and doubt"* can be used to help you clear any habit you have identified within yourself that you are trying to correct. To give you some examples and replace them with the habit that is relevant to you: *"I AM free from jealousy"* or *"I AM surrendering lust."* Or you can experiment with *"I AM replacing hatred with love."*

12

Wisdom Unlocked: Gaining Profound Insights

So what is wisdom, you ask?

At the time of writing this book, a search on Google led me to the *Collins Dictionary* where it states *'Wisdom is the ability to use your experience and knowledge in order to make sensible decisions or judgments.'*

Nevertheless, rather than chasing experience and knowledge, let us focus on chasing the wisdom given to us by our inner self.

The wisdom we receive once we fully surrender our minds and hold faith in our hearts to give us the right advice every time we turn to our inner self for guidance.

It's time we stop jumping into solving problems hastily, step back, and wait for the ripples to settle so we can see the answer clearly before we try to take things on.

Everything we have gone through together in this book so far has been preparing you for this next chapter on how to access the wisdom from the higher mind of your inner self.

The wisdom in mindfulness

If you have taken aboard even 5% of the keys I've shared in the book so far, you should be seeing these little sequences of magical moments start to pop up around you daily, reminding you that you've found the truth to life.

- It could be something as simple as being taken in completely by joy, simply by listening to others as they converse around you.
- Or it could be you are being lifted up by the invigorating breaths you take, changing your state completely, while outside walking with nature.
- Maybe it's the feeling of the warm and comforting sun shining above you, lifting you up and taking you into its heart.
- Or perhaps it's simply the kindness you start seeing in others as you witness them intentionally going out of their way to help you.

We're approaching a fork in the road ahead of us, one in where we faced to choose which path to take from here: either the one living a life within our minds or the one living a life within our hearts.

Looking at both of the paths in front of us, we know the one where we live a life within our hearts is the 'right' path.

No pun intended, right?

In our time together, I am certain you can see some truth within my words; I know you can, you can feel it in your heart.

To summarize this book in one sentence would be: *'Our heart is what holds the keys to the kingdom.'*

The kingdom of life... The kingdom of love... I know I am constantly labelling the feelings of these experiences of being connected with everything as being love, but it's the only emotion that comes close to explaining its majestic nature.

Guys... There is nothing emasculating about that.

Once you start noticing this shift for yourself, when you begin stepping in between these two worlds, it's truly magical. The littlest things around you start to lighten up your day, prompting you and reminding you, to bring your focus back to your heart.

If this starts happening to you, do not ignore it. Otherwise, you'll lose it. Be grateful for this 'other thing' that is stepping in to help you. It's now becoming more than just your daily alarms that are bringing you back to realign and attune with everything.

You start to see:

- *The perfection in nature.*
- *The perfection in aligning to love.*
- *The perfection that shines through the sun above us.*
- *The perfection within yourself, as you are already perfect when you're connected to your heart.*
- *Then, the perfection within your inner self.*

We are now beginning to walk the world thought-free and childlike.

All that is needed from here is for us to let go and hand the reins over to our inner self to lead, that's all we have to do.

This is the last piece of the puzzle to create the perfect picture of you 'living happily ever after.'

Once you let go of this sense of self and raise up into the higher levels of your heart, you won't need to read my words anymore; you'll always be connected to this world I speak of.

From here, I want you to start surrendering the outer things in the world around you that you look at to your inner self. Every time you look at others around you, your friends and loved ones, the meal you are about to eat, any pleasure you have in the world, surrender it to your inner self or the flame within your heart and then continue participating in whatever it is you are doing. This will help you begin integrating another dimension in how you live in the world and how you experience life.

If you can become completely co-dependent on this inner self within and above you and completely surrender all attachment to the outer world around you, this will take you even further in self-mastery than many others who have dedicated their whole lives to religion or a spiritual discipline.

It's not a competition, though, it's just what needs to be done.

Settle the waters and still your mind

The truth and meaning of life are simple once you stop and actually look.

How come when you are roaming through the forest, it's only when you sit down and stop for a moment and wait that the animals start appearing and showing themselves?

Think beyond yourself for a second as being the doer of everything. That is just your tyrant ego yelling, "look at me, me, me!"

Do you think if you stopped letting it steal all your attention and pointing at itself and how great it is, it would start fading away and cease to exist?

All the meditations and exercises on mindfulness, emptying yourself by listening gracefully, and aligning your heart and emotions to flow with the currents of love have all become the stepping stones for you to now step across into a new reality.

A new reality where you find this sense of awareness, in which your heart becomes like a window into a higher place where you can see the most beautiful set of eyes smiling down at you...

Is this the real you?

Is this your inner self?

Just a thought...

Maybe this is how it happens?

The fact is, the more we continue living life thought-free, with our feelings in harmony, the more we are preparing ourselves to receive this next level of inner guidance.

So give your all to conquer the flaws within yourself, and in return, you'll receive the keys to the kingdom.

It will happen; that's a promise.

The only thing that could be stopping you from receiving the keys right now is that your mind is still focused on the outer over the inner levels of your heart. Keep surrendering your outer self daily to your inner self above, and watch the layers peel away until only your real self remains, revealing the core truth of who you truly are.

Another trick to still your mind

If you're still having trouble quieting your mind despite trying the exercises in the previous chapters, let's take a new approach.

If you purchased this book to calm your mind, I will do everything I can to ensure you get what you paid for.

The next one is so simple yet so powerful; it works by using the power of focus.

There was a famous pearl of wisdom shared by a Zen buddhist saying:

"It is the space between the notes that makes the music."

On my own personal journey, I found a parallel to this Zen quote when a teacher and dear friend of mine suggested that rather than focusing on the thoughts themselves, start focusing on the space between the thoughts.

Think about that for a second.

Then, think about it again.

Now, look at the space between the two and focus on it.

Then, hold your focus on the space and get comfortable as you keep reading.

When we find ourselves being bombarded with recurring thoughts and persistently thinking, if we are focusing on our thoughts and keep reacting to them, all we are going to do is attract more thoughts.

Next time you are near a main road, I want you to stand and watch it for a while and watch the cars drive by.

See the cars as being your thoughts crossing your mind.

You won't hang on to each car and let it rip you down the road, would you?

Yet, this is what we are doing in our minds.

Just because a thought crosses the screen of your mind, it doesn't mean you have to react. Just observe and accept it, then shift your focus to the space or the spaces between the thoughts you are having.

Now that you are focused on the space between your thoughts, all of a sudden, the space between your thoughts starts expanding, almost as if your mind is similar to a camera lens, focusing on that space while the thoughts you were having start fading out of focus.

Even if thoughts are still surfacing, because you are not focusing on them and only focusing on the space between, you're going to attract more space, leading the thoughts to fade away to nothing.

By concentrating and holding our attention on the space between our thoughts, our minds start opening up, filling our minds with more emptiness.

Do you get it?

- *It feels so good once you find that space and see it.*
- *You can start to daydream now, focusing on nothing but that space.*
- *Take a break for a moment, you need it.*
- *Congratulations, you have just intentionally stopped your mind.*

It's funny; they say our brain is like a muscle, which means we have been going to the gym every day non-stop for years, but it's not until you've shut it up that we can finally have a rest day.

You can now continue looking at this space, holding a quiet mind for as long as you choose to, and repeat the process whenever need to if you ever need to bring yourself back to this emptiness.

For the rest of your life! Finally!

I hope this book has now paid for itself.

Every time you see the thoughts come creeping back in, remember, it's because you're focusing on your thoughts and not the space.

Simple. All you need to do is bring your focus back to the space between your thoughts, watch the space start magnifying and saddle that horse to stop your mental body from galloping away in front of you.

This here is an active meditation that you can now add to your arsenal.

If you want to dig a little deeper, start to listen gracefully to that space between the thoughts and tell me what you hear.

There are deeper levels of silence that only the diligent will find...

If you have any issues stilling your mind at all, give this exercise three times today and three times tomorrow and watch how far you have come in two days to conquer this issue for good.

Remember, practice makes professionals.

I trust this will serve you well.

Find your inner teacher, your inner self

Have you ever gone to leave the house and heard this soft, still voice in your heart telling you, *"Take a jacket"* or *"Take an umbrella"*, yet you still ignored or disobeyed it because it appeared the weather was fine?

Then you find yourself caught in the weather, thinking to yourself, why didn't I listen to that voice?

This was your inner self.

This was your inner self talking to you.

If you practice listening to this voice and follow it, you will never make the wrong decision again.

This voice knows the answer to every single problem you will ever have, and to this day, I say, with full conviction, that it has never told me the wrong thing to do or say, even when it was extremely hard for me to accept what it had asked me to do.

So how do we build a closer relationship with this inner self within us who is also our inner teacher?

Let us look into it a little more, shall we?

Ask the question and wait

At any moment in our lives, whether reflecting in solitude or if problems fall upon us in the moment, we must make decisions and ask our hearts:

"What should I do?"

or *"What should I say?"*

After asking, surrender completely and wait for an answer.

When you find yourself in a situation where others are present and you need to act straight away, ensure that your actions are guided by love. When you act with love, your decisions are typically wiser, less selfish, and better received by those around you, as love has the power to influence everything.

Rock, paper, scissors, love.

Love beats all.

It's funny, to this day, sometimes I get the answer to what I have asked immediately, but sometimes it takes time for me to get it. That doesn't phase me, though, as the more you practice listening and acting with the guidance of your inner self, the more you'll see every decision you make as being the right one.

Every decision, how cool is that?

This takes some time and only happens after a while; remember, we are playing the long game here. It took me almost forty years of living and learning before I started to obey and listen to my inner self more consistently. So, if this is your first time reading, don't stress too much on this part.

Please note: *This part will make a lot more sense once those reading it have disciplined their thoughts and feelings to be still and quiet and have aligned their four lower bodies and led them into the shining white pearl I mentioned in earlier chapters.*

The most important point I could make in this book that is above all else in this book is this point here... Listen.

'Life becomes so much easier when you learn to obey and follow the guidance of your inner self.'

So make a game of it.

Create a reward system for yourself; that's what I did.

Every time you are asked to do something, and you listen and do it, once you complete the task you were asked to do, clench your hand into a fist and whisper to your inner self, *"Victory!"*

These little micro-wins of celebrating will keep you on the ultimate goal we are looking to achieve, and that is to completely mirror your inner self, looking up to it with love and adoration as we follow and obey its guidance and continue serving all life around us.

Obey the prompting

Once you get the answer to what to do, please do it. It's that simple.

I will tell you from experience that whatever your inner self says is the right thing to do it's the right thing to do.

I disobeyed it for many years and managed to mentally justify to myself the reasons why I was disobeying it, as if I was selling myself the wisdom in my choices.

By persuading others, we convince ourselves.

I know I'd probably be in a different place in life right now if I learned to obey it from day one. This is a personal journey, though; everyone has their own stuff to work through and their own blocks within themselves they have to break.

Sacrifice, surrender, selflessness, and service to others are the four keys you must practice if you truly want to break through these blocks in yourself.

Another angle that may help is whenever your inner self gives you an order that you know you don't want to follow, ask yourself, "What if?"

Remember, this is the moment where you are at the fork in the road we were at before. Your heart is telling you to go this way, and your mind is telling you to go the other way, so make a choice.

If you choose your mind, cast your vision into the future, and ponder on what if?

What if I make the decision to act from my heart or act for myself?

Think about the words I just used there for a second...

Sacrifice, surrender, selflessness, and service.

Now, do what you need to do and watch the scenes of life unfold, and at the end of the scene, if you find yourself caught in a pickle, reflect back to the moment you chose to follow

206

yourself and not your heart, and if the moment could have been any different if you acted on what you were asked to do.

You won't always be able to tell, but sometimes you will.

This is probably the first step we can take on the path of self-correction.

I know this is a lot to take in.

Just absorb the words I am saying and the lesson I am giving as you are listening to it on more than one level.

Full disclaimer: Your inner self will never tell you to do any harm to yourself or bring any harm to another person. If you are getting any suggestions of this, that is not your inner self, I promise you. The more you pursue love, the more you'll be able to discern the difference between your inner self and your mind or anything else.

It is a gift to not know the answer to something

Have you ever been in a conversation with someone where you're trying to remember the name of something or someone, and you can't remember for some reason, yet it's on the tip of your tongue, and then you start getting frustrated at yourself?

Then, as soon as you walk away from the conversation, or you're driving in the car, the answer pops into your mind, and you're like, that's it!

Have you ever had that?

I am sure everyone has, and that's because the mind doesn't function very well under stress.

Yet, so many people are super hard on themselves when they get stuck on a problem or issue that they don't know the answer to.

The first thing for us to take away from this is that the mind never works well under stress, so don't even try.

The next thing that will take your understanding to a whole new level is that whenever the mind doesn't know the answer to a problem, it will send you into meditation.

"Got ya monkey mind!"

Hmm... So, is this why people get angry when they don't know the answer to something?

Yes, and that's because the monkey mind knows a state of meditation is coming...

Here is why.

When you are constantly running laps in your head of recurring memories, constantly processing and answering problems with ease, your monkey mind is holding the steering wheel. Nonetheless, when a problem comes in that it can't solve within the memory of what it already knows, then the mind breaks free from the shackles of being in memory and moves from being in a loop of memory back into the current moment.

Now, we are in the moment...

The mind is in a state of not knowing the answer and is searching for something to grab onto, but there is nothing for it to grab.

It's now caught in the space between the thoughts...

And how good is this space?!

Like meditation, it is also an expansive feeling... It feels just so awesome not knowing the answer to something.

I believe all the Zen literature was focused towards bringing us out of our minds and back into this space between our thoughts.

When we break free from being caught in memory, we use the power of focus to focus on the space between our thoughts and practice getting on with our lives. Meaning that we are now re-training ourselves to operate with and have an empty mind.

This is the next level again.

- *You become more sensitive to your inner self when it guides you, as your not drowned out in thought.*
- *Your mind isn't running the show now, narrating about everything, blinding you from life, and even interactions with others around you become so much more special.*
- *You may even notice that because your head is quiet and clear, your inner vision opens up more, allowing you to see more of these inner planes above you to start to open up around you.*

So, next time you don't know the answer to something or what you should do in a situation, and you've already asked your inner self a question but haven't received an answer, rather than finding yourself falling into a pit of frustration, I'll break down what you need to do.

Firstly, see it. Then know it's got you, and you don't know the answer.

Secondly, surrender. Admit the problem has you, and you can't resolve the issue yourself.

Thirdly, ask your inner self again for the answer.

Then finally, enjoy the unknown. Use the paragraphs above to help you understand how to really master these moments through the test you're facing.

1) See it.

2) *Surrender.*
3) *Ask your inner self.*
4) *Enjoy the unknown.*

Remember, you have this unshakable faith within your heart, knowing the answer will come to you shortly. Until then, enjoy the moment.

Please note: When I speak about memory in this section, I refer to everything you already know analytically or anything that has already happened. If you take pride in knowing the answer to everything or are stuck in the past, reminiscing on the golden years of your life, this section is for you.

Talk to your heart

When you're driving home from work or driving to get dinner or something, don't just jump on the phone to speak with someone about how good or bad your day was.

Why not experiment by trying to talk with your inner self?

- Whether it's out loud or in your heart, tell them about your problems.
- Then, try sharing with them everything you are excited about, especially with what you're incorporating into your days with this book.
- Thank them for the moments you have seen today and how they have helped you. *(This part here is super important.)*

It may feel a little crazy at first, but when you take the plunge and just start talking, you will feel a great weight lifted off your shoulders. You can sense your inner self is listening, it's a similar feeling to when you are venting out to a true friend, and you can feel their concern and love.

What are you fixated on? Observe your surroundings

Are you noticing your mind is focusing and fixating on all the wrong things?

We can waste a lot of energy through overthinking and visualizing excessively. Observe your surroundings: the music you are listening to and the videos you are watching on your phone and on TV. refining what is around you can help soften your fixations a little.

Again, this is something you may not need to change in your world immediately, but in time, you may need to start dropping some of these temporal pleasures to refine your mind so you can start to step up higher.

We have been desensitized so much by TV these days. If you watch any movie on Netflix, the majority of society is able to watch someone be murdered or hurt in a movie or TV show and have no emotional response, like we have become a bunch of desensitized robots ingesting this poison from The Matrix.

Unplug yourself to step up higher. The less rubbish you feed your ears and vision, the more these inner planes of higher consciousness will start opening up for you.

Re-read this book often

If you have found even a couple of things in this book that will help you in your day-to-day life, please read or listen to this book again, say, in three to six months from now. As I mentioned earlier, I have written this book purposely to give you more than one reading worth of content.

I openly admit that it may take some time before you chew your food with all of the cosmos.

The next time you read or listen to this, you will hear new things you never picked up or overlooked the first time reading. Even if the second time reading, you only find another two or three tools that help you break through that next block in your life at the time will keep you rising higher on the path and continue to grow as a person.

Careful of criticism, condemnation, & judgment

Criticism, condemnation, and judgment are some of the biggest blocks to your inner self. Maybe it is because it takes us outside of the circle of oneness with everything, or maybe it's something else. It's something I want you to be aware of, so whenever you are finding it hard to connect with your inner self, at least you'll be able to monitor your patterns closely and see if there is any connection.

This is what I have found personally, so I would assume this goes for you as well. We are all even here. Identify and reflect if you've done something wrong, but don't beat yourself up for it, as that will get you nowhere.

Rome wasn't built in a day, so be patient with yourself. As soon as you feel that something is wrong when you start doing it, know you're already halfway there to overcome it. You got this!

Spend more time in the secret chamber of your heart

I spoke before on meditating on the electric blue plume of fire in the secret chamber of your heart to increase your mastery in power. Next to the blue plume of flame on the left, the center flame is a dazzling golden plume that symbolizes wisdom. If you ever feel you're not progressing within yourself, this is the flame you need to turn to.

This is the flame to focus on and nurture.

Be mindful that the three flames above the shining white pearl have to grow together, and if you haven't mastered one of the three, the other two are held back until you master the one you have the least mastery in.

Let us see the dazzling, golden yellow flame dancing and pulsing to our heartbeat as we see the yellow fire clear our mind, give us greater clarity on every challenge we are facing, and bring our mind closer to being able to see and hear our inner self more clearly.

Even before starting your car and driving, you could even close your eyes for 20 seconds to see your inner child, dressed in white, opening the wooden doors and sitting before these flames above the shining white pearl.

Open your eyes and start driving while still focusing within. Use your imagination and start getting creative in the ways you can spend more time in this secret chamber, for the more time you spend in here, the more you'll see a new freedom open to you.

Reflection exercise: surrender unto s greater love

For this reflection exercise, let us work together to surrender the outer world to inner world even more, as I want to make sure you understand this clearly. Once you get this part of my book, all the other areas will start coming to you really easily, and it will also help you let go whenever you are struggling with anything.

The first time we go through this, there will be a longer process to it. However, once you understand and have done it several times, you can easily surrender your attention to anything around you that you can see.

By putting your inner self before all outer distractions, it brings you into an even deeper union with your inner self.

To all the champions who are reading this book, I invite you to incorporate this ritual into the five reminders you've set on your phone to help you reconnect throughout the day. After realigning yourself, take a moment to observe the people and objects around you. Focus on them and surrender them to your inner self. This will add another layer of oneness to your everyday life. We have spent most of our lives prioritizing the external world over our inner selves. Let's start correcting this now.

You have set yourself those five daily reminders, haven't you?

All good, just checking ;)

Take a seat for a moment and close your eyes. Focus on nothing but your breath. Center yourself until you are completely comfortable and in your native state. Visualize a small version of yourself, the size of a thumb, clothed in white, running up a spiral staircase that leads you into your heart.

You push open the big wooden doors and enter into the secret chamber within your heart.

You sit or kneel before the shining white pearl and three colored flames in the center of the room and begin breathing in the white fire within the pearl. Hold in your breath for a moment, then breathe out into the pearl and flame to invigorate the blue, yellow, and pink flames and bring them into balance and expand.

They pulse and dance to the cadences of your heartbeat. You feel the desire now to enter into the pearl, so you step into the pearl, which lifts you up with a surge of the three flames expanding.

You open your eyes and can see everything around you, only a little bit lighter and brighter. This is your inner self, which is an extension of the three flames that are pulsing within your heart.

Now open your eyes and look around you at everything you can see.

Whatever your outer self locks onto, let it go and surrender it passing it to your inner self above you.

This then replaces your perception of whatever it is your looking at, from seeing it independently to seeing it co-existent with your inner self.

Take a moment to focus on the objects in the room: chairs, tables, furniture, people, cars, mobile phones. Imagine each item rising up and being surrendered to your inner self. By doing this, you are releasing yourself from a purely physical perspective and opening up to higher levels of consciousness.

Continue scanning the room, surrendering everything you see – even the book you're reading and the ground beneath you. Keep doing this until you begin to create a new reality where there is nothing separating you from your inner self.

Once you have surrendered everything in the room, step outside and repeat the process. If going outside isn't an option, move to another room in your house and surrender everything you can see to your inner self.

If you are outside, surrender the plants, trees, and any animals you see, then observe the shift in vibration as you enter into a new state of consciousness.

Keep surrendering everything you can see until you can't surrender anymore.

- Now, notice the state you have entered into.
- You have just heightened your consciousness with your eyes open.
- You have now learned how to raise your consciousness through an active meditation.
- Look at every object around you that you have surrendered onto your inner self.
- They are not just physical objects anymore, they are now etheric or formless as well.
- Can you turn up the light in them and make them brighter?
- Can you hold your focus, even if it's just for two minutes, on the etheric version of everything around you?
- Just like when we focused on the space between thoughts earlier, can we zoom in on the etheric and let the physical version around us?
- Can we repeat the process again, surrendering everything around us and elevating the world even higher?

This is one of my favorite parts of life. If you understand this, in my eyes you have made it.

I am literally shaking your hand right now, congratulating you that you've made it to this point.

Remember this: for anything to exist in the physical world, it must also exist on higher planes. Your inner self is the vehicle that can help you reach these higher planes. Whenever something or someone moves you, surrender it to your inner self and watch as this integration of spiritual realms takes you higher and higher. This applies to both the positive and negative aspects of life. Nothing can stand between you and your inner self. Let go of everything and rise higher. Your inner self is like a hot air balloon lifting you to higher levels of consciousness, while external distractions are like sandbags holding you down. Release every outer distraction you have and watch yourself ascend.

Meditation exercise: our inner self

For this meditation, we can either be sitting or standing, whichever you prefer.

Close your eyes, and bring your energies into the center of your heart through your breath.

You walk into the secret chamber within the hidden recesses of your heart and sit down before the shining white pearl in the center of the room and gaze upon the three flames above the pearl, pulsing in unison to the rhythm of your heart.

You breathe in the fire and spirit from the pearl as you breathe in, holding it in and letting the life force within your lungs spread all through your body and charge every cell of your being.

You breathe out with a slow, deliberate breath to ignite the plumes dancing in unison.

You repeat the same breath again, this time slower... breathing in and holding... Then, breathing out onto the pearl and flame; seeing the blue, yellow, and pink plumes of flame intertwine and balance.

They start spinning together.

The white light from the pearl starts lighting the room and turns to a white fire that merges with the flame above it, making it shine pearlescent with blue, yellow, and pink tinges to the shine of the white fire.

The room gets brighter and brighter as this fire grows and fills the room.

Within the center of the fire, a figure appears out of the shining white pearl.

You can barely see their outline besides their crystal blue eyes looking deeply at you because it is so bright.

You send them love and recognize them, even though you can see them clearly.

Rather than trying to visualize them precisely, all you see is their outline.

You can see their garment shimmering with the same pearlescent white as the fire that has filled the room.

The fire starts to fade down, bringing your eyes to adjust and see your inner self stepping towards you.

Your inner self stops, sending the most comforting love through their eyes to you.

You look at them and your understanding of everything starts increasing.

The highest vision of yourself is contained within this inner self.

You desire no other image other than this inner self.

You kneel before them, thanking your heart with gratitude that they have descended to meet you personally.

Your inner self stands before you, reaching their arm out and touching your forehead gracefully and transferring the most incredible love that takes every burden of weight off of you, causing you to almost cry in relief.

You open your heart to them and speak with them, sharing anything that is weighing you down right now, confessing and surrendering anything that is stopping you from raising up with them.

You may now ask them a question if you choose.

If they don't answer, just smile and wait, knowing already that even communing in silence with them is teaching you so much.

You may open your eyes when you feel it is time to end the meditation.

If you choose to journal your experience, you can.

If you do, ask your inner self to help you write what you need to write.

Things to consider

This reflective exercise of surrendering everything around us to our inner self is extremely important. Once you have completed it thoroughly from start to finish, you can then quickly realign yourself and bring yourself closer to your inner self and the higher levels of consciousness above you whenever you choose.

Throughout your entire life, you have been perceiving the things around you through your mind. By projecting your thoughts onto the objects or things you see, you have created a barrier between yourself and your inner self. We need to unravel this, and this exercise will help you to uncover years of self-created barriers.

When you surrender the outer world to your inner self and let it take control, something remarkable happens. This experience is something you should explore for yourself, watching it unfold personally. Constant surrendering will free you from all attachment, pain, desires, and the overwhelming feelings we get from trying to cling to the outer world and its material possessions.

Remember to practice the meditation on your inner self consistently, even if it's just before falling asleep in bed. You can include the inner self in any of your previous meditation practices by visualizing a shining white pearl and three flames above it. Focus on the shining white pearl, blue, yellow, and pink flames, and the inner self as all being connected and the same thing.

You can imagine entering a secret chamber within your heart and communicating with your inner self, whether you visualize the inner self directly in front of you or speak to the pearl and flames, knowing that they are all connected.

The meditation exercise is an effective and powerful practice that helps strengthen our connection to our inner selves. You can visualize them descending into your heart and standing before you. This can be added to the end of any meditation in this book for an extra layer if you like. You can also combine any of the meditations in this book to create your own personalized practice. That's the main goal here. I've included a diverse range of meditations to give you options. I hope you find one that resonates with you and continue to practice it daily.

Please note: *Anyone reading this book which is religious or holds a background in a particular faith can also experiment with seeing their inner self as being Jesus, Krishna, Gautama Buddha, or any other spiritual figure who holds a mantle in the faith you follow.*

I am sure they have raised to a level where they can still descend into the recesses of your heart. Try the meditation again, but see them entering in instead of your inner self.

13

Unity in Diversity: Realizing We Are All One

This chapter will explore the concept of experiencing a sense of oneness often discussed in Eastern religions. It's important to know that feeling a sense of oneness does not require any specific religion. I plan to explore this theme more deeply, which will help enhance your understanding and make it easier for you to achieve this state.

During meditation, we can connect deeply with everything around us by closing our eyes and silencing our sense of self. This helps us enter a state of oneness and feel more connected.

We have already experienced the truth of oneness through meditation. Let's focus on feeling this same sense of oneness while interacting with the world rather than just experiencing it during meditation.

Let us look at several strategies to help us constantly stay connected with everything.

Ultimately, our ego and sense of self are the greatest barriers to experiencing oneness. If we can effectively erase this sense of self, we will become like a sugar cube dropping into water:

the illusion of self we have built will dissolve, and then we will become part of something bigger. Let's explore some ways in which we can achieve this.

The four pillars to oneness

The main philosophy of this book is to help establish a series of daily prompts that will help us re-establish our connection and realign ourselves.

Our main objective is to achieve mindfulness and connection for extended periods of time and work towards spending more time in a mindful state until it becomes our usual state. Eventually, we will be less reliant on prompts to stay connected and will be able to consistently maintain a sense of oneness with everything. The following four points of focus will serve as your four pillars to oneness, as the more you concentrate on them, the more they will help you remain in this state.

1) Listening Gracefully

The key to achieving a sense of oneness is practicing graceful listening. I initially introduced the concept of graceful listening in the early chapters because it is a powerful tool for calming a restless mind, soothing emotional turmoil, and focusing on what is outside of ourselves. This helps us break free from the limitations imposed by our ego.

Setting daily alarms to remind ourselves to practice silent listening was a strategy to help us strengthen our ability to quiet our minds and make graceful listening a natural part of our daily routine.

The ultimate goal is to be able to practice graceful listening continuously. As you progress towards oneness, it is important to focus on the peaceful pauses of silence and listen to them as if searching for sounds behind them, leading you to experience a more profound sense of emptiness.

Once we become more comfortable with this type of listening, we start to expect and appreciate the moments of silence as they appear and begin to listen for deeper meaning. Training yourself to focus on listening and to seek out the sounds behind the moments of silence is similar in a sense to practicing meditation. It can enable you to deeply connect with a sense of oneness at any time of the day. Focusing on this practice is essential because when we listen this way, we are not engaging in internal dialogues that reinforce our sense of self. Our ego and identity often act as barriers, preventing us from aligning with everything and experiencing oneness. When we truly listen, we are fully present, and our attention is directed outward, allowing us to connect and align ourselves with our surroundings and experience a greater sense of emptiness, which leads us then to oneness.

2) Align yourself with nature

Please take a moment to acknowledge the nature around you. When you see a tree or a bush, focus on it and follow its branches down to the trunk, then to its roots and into the ground below. Next, send love through your feet into the ground below you, just as we did in the previous grounding exercise to establish a connection with the earth beneath us. Once you feel connected to the ground, visualize a connection between the ground beneath you and the ground beneath the tree. Hold this connection while expanding your heart to surround the tree with love. When you feel comfortable and aligned with the tree, you can repeat this process with every other tree, bush, and blade of grass around you until you feel connected with every part of nature surrounding you.

This exercise might seem like a stretch at first, but after a couple of repetitions, you'll naturally trace the trees to their roots and connect to the ground almost automatically.

If you see birds or animals, look into their eyes and realize that love is guiding and controlling them. This exercise is especially helpful with animals you are scared of. However, never put yourself in danger. I am not in any way suggesting that you go and try to hug a mountain lion or grizzly bear! Start with animals like dogs, cats, birds, and squirrels. With birds, it's beneficial to observe them and understand that love is guiding and controlling them. Then, listen to their chirping. Can you see how, by integrating love into our senses, we are starting to build the foundations of oneness?

Any opportunity you have the chance to connect yourself with nature, take it. As you spend more time focusing on this, you will start doing it without even realizing it, and it will become more automatic. Then, in time, you will always be connected with nature, and by doing so, you will be mirroring its vibration. This vibration connects you to everything and brings you a sense of oneness. Remember that.

3) Oneness in the shining white pearl

Every meditation I've discussed has involved visualizing a shining white pearl. Why?

Focusing on the shining white pearl helps bring our energy inward and prevents it from being scattered by external distractions. This centers our four lower bodies, allowing us to step up higher.

Initially, prioritize focusing on the shining white pearl above everything else. If you are consistent with this, you will feel a constant connection to your inner self and the secret star above in time. For now, concentrating on the shining white pearl should be your primary focus.

Once you've mastered the practice of graceful listening, shift your focus to listening from your ears to within the center of the shining white pearl.

When connecting with nature and the ground below you, try holding that connection, entering the recesses of your heart, walking into the shining white pearl, and stepping forward, like you are walking on the ground from within this higher dimension. If you do this often, it will accelerate your connection to nature.

You've already established three pillars by listening and connecting with nature through the shining white pearl. With continued focus, you will notice significant progress within just a few days, leading to a fundamental reprogramming of yourself that will make it difficult to revert to your previous ways before picking up and reading this book. The more consistent you are with this, the more this process becomes second nature.

Next, let's break down the remaining barrier: our division with others.

There have been wedges put between yourself and others since you were a child. Fortunately for you, this has all been forged on your outer self, so if you are connected to your inner self, those wedges have no place anymore. When I say wedges, I mean ambition, competition, lust, pride, fear, and all those things sewn in your psyche to make you push harder and climb as an individual.

When you look at others around you, visualize a shining white pearl within their hearts. If you look at that, you won't be blinded by the division of this world; and you'll be looking towards their inner essence, which will also help them connect to their inner self.

We have spent much time focused on the shining white pearl within our hearts; now it is time to start seeing it in others. If you visualize a shining white pearl within the center of their chest, do so. If not, just know it's there. Try to look at the shining white pearl within their hearts rather than looking at their outer appearance. Once you visualize this or are focused on it, send love to the pearl within their hearts. Even if you are holding eye contact and conversing with them, your internal focus is on that point of the shining white pearl. So when you speak to them now, this is not an outer discussion but a transfer of your love, wisdom, and power directly to their spiritual core. It's almost like your heart was a candle, and you've stretched out and lit a candle within their hearts.

If you choose to take on this part, you'll experience conversations that take both of you to higher dimensions of consciousness, even if neither of you can see it with your outer awareness.

It might sound a bit far-fetched, but I found this a helpful tool. By seeing others around me as shining white pearls and focusing more on their inner dimensions rather than their outer appearances, I was able to counter my habit of criticizing and judging others. This approach also helped me overcome the negative influence of lust, which was another issue I struggled with.

That's right, I have had my own challenges, just like every-one else.

Overcoming the tendency to criticize and judge others is tough, but it's a significant barrier to personal growth.

Both seeing the shining white pearl within others and count-ing to three have been the most effective tools for me to significantly reduce this tendency to criticize and judge.

4) Keep surrendering constantly

Your following key to finding oneness is through surrendering. When we surrender, we are letting go of all our attachment to something and surrendering ourselves. Whenever you find yourself wanting something, surrender it. Whether you engage in the activity or not is irrelevant; this will help you stay connected to your inner self and those higher levels more, as your desires and habits aren't pulling you away from your spiritual center as much. Give it all to your inner self. Any problem you have in your world, surrender it. Anytime you feel any emotion or anything you don't like, surrender it. This doesn't mean the problem will go away; it just means that even if it's still there, it's not just you addressing the problem; you have invited your inner self into your world more to help you. Through surrendering, you put yourself within a white pillar of light, and nothing can touch or rattle you now because it has nothing to cling onto because you've surrendered it.

This is your ticket to freedom. If you embody the virtue and habit of being able to surrender effortlessly, you'll still face problems in life, but you'll be able to drop them with ease. This means surrendering them so you're not carrying them and bogging yourself down.

By gracefully listening and continually aligning and connecting ourselves to nature, placing the white pearl within our hearts and others before everything else, and relinquishing any sense of struggle outside of ourselves, we can attain a deeper understanding of oneness and lead more fulfilling lives because we've built the four pillars to oneness.

Understanding the ego

To achieve a greater sense of oneness, we must recognize that the oneness we seek lies within our native state. In earlier chapters, I introduced the concept that through meditation, we naturally return to our native state after silencing our thoughts. This leads us to the idea that we are always in our native state, and our thoughts, feelings, and outer awareness are what cloud us from sensing and entering it.

During meditation, as we silence ourselves and sense ourselves returning to our native state, we experience a feeling of expansiveness, which connects us to everything around us and opens us up to that sense of oneness.

Often, when we open our eyes again, we fall back into our old ways and unconsciously go back to seeing ourselves as separate individuals rather than feeling a sense of oneness. This happens because we revert to the self-identity we've been developing since childhood - our ego. Our ego, or self-image, keeps us from feeling connected to everything. Letting go of our ego will allow us to experience a greater sense of oneness.

Simple enough?

Before we move forward, it's important to understand and resolve problems, so let's do it!

The following perspective might not apply to everyone, and

that's okay. You don't have to adopt it, but I recommend reading on. Some people are okay with living based on their ego, and that's fine. I'm not saying you have to change. My role is to present information, and you can decide what's right for you. I encourage you to read on to better understand yourself and others. Recognizing ego patterns can help you approach situations with more empathy and compassion in the future. Remember that almost everyone has an ego to some extent, which affects our actions and reactions. Recognizing ego behaviours in others can help you react with more compassion, so pay attention to this section.

Please note: I am an enthusiast in this field, not a professional. I am sharing general advice that has helped me overcome this obstacle personally, and I encourage you to research this topic further if you are interested in learning more.

What is the ego?

There are numerous misconceptions about our ego and what it represents. I would define it as a construct that we have created to shape our self-identity. It significantly influences how we perceive and react to the world around us. Once understood, overcoming it is a similar process for everyone, regardless of their ego's size.

From a young age, we learn to develop our sense of self by observing and imitating our parents and siblings. The inter-actions and relationships we have during childhood greatly influence our self-worth and feelings of security, contributing to the development of our ego. As we grow older, societal values, educational experiences, and life events all play a role in shaping our ego and sense of self. The stories we believe about ourselves and share further strengthen this self-concept, and the labels we give ourselves, such as "smart," "kind," "funny," and "successful," all contribute to solidifying our identity.

Our first priority is understanding the ego and how it affects our thoughts and actions. Before we can work on overcoming its influence, we need to explore its different aspects.

We should let go of the idea of self that limits our ability to feel connected with others. The idea of being a separate person is like trying to confine our entire consciousness within the boundaries of our skull. I mean, we have expanded our consciousness through meditation and reflective exercises, haven't we?

The first step to overcoming the ego is realizing it is something we have created and not a fixed identity. Letting go of the ego doesn't mean we are losing our identity but shedding the lesser self to embrace the greater self. By dissolving the identity we have formed to connect with the external world, we can then establish a greater unity and interdependence with our inner self.

The problem with our ego

Our ego can cause problems by separating us from others and our surroundings. It can also hold us back from personal growth, emotional well-being, and good relationships. The ego hides our true self behind a made-up identity and stops us from reaching our full potential. It creates a false sense of self-based on outside things like achievements, possessions, and social status. This can make us feel like we are not connected to

others, leading to feelings of loneliness, isolation, and discon-
nection. The ego also tends to judge and compare, making us
feel superior and leading to envy, resentment, and division. It
pushes us to compete by holding on to material things, status,
and relationships for validation. The ego is never satisfied
and always wants more, which can lead to suffering. It is
focused on keeping control and protecting itself from threats,
often leading to fear, anxiety, and resistance to change. When
someone is ego-centered, their ability to understand others
and see things from their point of view is limited, making
them narrow-minded. The ego also overreacts to criticism
and failure, making it hard for us to learn and accept feedback.
It constantly wants validation and often keeps us from being in
the present moment. Additionally, the ego can distort reality,
stopping us from growing spiritually and feeling a sense of
oneness, peace, and enlightenment.

I understand that this section contains a lot of information.
Still, it's important to recognize the impact the ego has in
preventing us from completing our divine plan. Understanding
the ego is the first step towards realizing its influence on us
in our daily lives. By taking steps to transcend this part of
ourselves, we can experience greater peace, fulfilment, and
connection with others and the world, as overcoming the ego
can make life more enjoyable and easier, not just for ourselves
but also for everyone around us.

Defense Mechanisms for the ego

When you start acting on this and taking steps to overcome the
ego, you begin to wrestle with a stubborn force that doesn't
want to change. It has many defense mechanisms to protect

itself. Learning every move it can make is important, so we can laugh at ourselves and others when we see it in action.

Here are a few actions and reactions of the ego, so you can see the cards it will play to stay hidden and protect itself.

1. It will refuse to accept things. Even when they are clearly explained or shown to you — for example, if you are in the wrong in a situation.
2. It will point out flaws in others, even ones you engage in, to distract you from making changes yourself.
3. It will self-justify and rationalize things to protect itself. For instance, if you make a wrong decision, you will rationalize your actions by sharing your reasons to lead you to believe your actions were right.
4. It will direct negative emotions towards someone or something and vent them out on a safer target. This could be something as simple as your partner wearing the stress you are carrying from work.
5. It will lead you to throw a tantrum like a child or overreact blowing up at others to get your way. This can mean giving your partner a hard time for making a big decision without you to punish them, being difficult with your friends if things don't go your way, or even blowing up at a barista if they mess up your order.
6. It will blind you intellectually to mask emotional stress or anxiety. Many people become workaholics to shield themselves from pain or stress at home. This is a defense mechanism of the ego.
7. It will take you off in flights of fantasy, playing out

situations where you are the hero in the story of a crisis. As stimulating as they may be, who is the one holding the camera at the end of the day?

8. It will lead you to engage in reckless behavior as a way to vent anger and frustration. Driving over the speed limit in your car or drinking excessively on the weekend are just two examples

9. It will push you to become fragile and constantly need validation. This can be recognition from your boss at work, your partner acknowledging the cleaning you've done around the house, or your friends noticing weight loss.

10. It will separate and isolate you from others to promote feelings of loneliness and isolation. Staying at home and going 'off the radar' to make yourself unreachable, or the feeling of boredom on a Friday night because you're at home and not going out. Not returning a phone call when someone is calling you because they are concerned for you, is another layer of the ego promoting a power struggle in which you think you're winning, but really, your ego is keeping you in isolation.

11. It will encourage you to point the finger and judge others, giving you a sense of superiority and inferiority. When you point your finger at someone, remember that there are three fingers pointing back at you. The second you look down at someone, your ego has the reins. So, take them back.

12. It will cling to your material possessions to validate itself. We've all done it or do it, that cool car, that pretty dress, those nice shoes promoting the image of success. It does nothing but lead to more suffering as you'll never satisfy

it, leading it to want more and more.

13. It will resist any change or growth as it sees change as a threat to its identity. That's right, you're not a procrastinator, it's the ego. Are you going to let this thing win? Get up and take action.

14. It will cloud your ability to see your inner self. The ego is one of the greatest enemies of the inner self, as it is always about "me, me, me!" trying to keep your eyes on it and not the shining white pearl. Remember to surrender your ego to your inner self daily.

15. If someone says something out of line or mean to you, it will hurt your feelings. If someone hurts your feelings, that is an ego reaction. Start observing this from now on, and you'll notice that often, the pain comes from the pit of your stomach. Start laughing at it more and commenting to yourself, "That was an ego reaction." Watch how quickly you can brush it off.

16. Your ego may even try to turn you off from this section of the book completely. Did you find yourself just scrolling over this part with your eyes and not reading it?

Someone's getting a little scared right now...

Maybe in this whole list?

If you can't see yourself doing any of these things, look at the first defence mechanism I mentioned.

Anytime you find yourself responding with irritation, blaming others, competing with others, judging others, boasting, feeling entitled, jealous, resentful, attention-seeking, or controlling others, it is also your ego in action.

Wow!

There is a lot we have to work on here! Rather than trying to tackle everything at once, I want you to take a step back and observe yourself as if you were a 'fly on the wall', paying attention to moments when things aren't going your way and see if your ego is starting influencing your daily interactions.

I suggest you revisit this chapter daily from here on and choose one point a day from the ego defense mechanisms I've mentioned, and see if you can see it surface within yourself or in others around you. Progress through all of the defense mechanisms in this step-by-step manner. Doing this will allow you to remember and recognize them more effectively when you encounter them in your behaviours and the behavoiurs of others.

The ego has various ways of protecting itself. Let's start by focusing on these defense mechanisms, as they are the behaviours that often make it the most difficult for someone to work with or interact with.

Please note: this information is for your eyes and your awareness, and it is for you to work on. If you start pointing the finger at other people's ego actions and reactions they will let you know about it. You can still call someone out on their actions; just don't say it was their ego acting.

The ego will do anything to protect itself, including letting loose on you and giving you a mouthful.

How to overcome the ego

Now that we have a better understanding of the ego's tactics, let's explore how to overcome it and ensure that we emerge victorious in the battle. The most important thing to remember is that surrendering this part of ourselves does not mean losing our identity. Everything we have learned and that has shaped us into who we are will remain with us; it's simply about letting go of the lesser self to become part of something greater.

Please note: The first rule is to focus on our inner self, which is also a part of our future self, as we visualized in the first chapters reflective exercise. This will help us to develop a new identity that replaces our ego or lesser self as we start surrendering it. It also provides us with a point of focus giving us something to surrender unto, which makes the process a lot easier. If you haven't reached the stage of sensing your inner self and aligning yourself, taking on the ego is not recommended, as it will often lead you to focus on your flaws and potentially put yourself in a negative spiral.

In saying that... Let us continue...

I want you to say this out aloud 3 times with me.

"I am surrendering my ego and all attachment I have to my ego onto my inner self."

That wasn't loud! Say it like you mean it.
  Again!

"I am surrendering my ego and all attachment I have to my ego onto my inner self!"

Can you feel that?!?
  You are going to beat this... And when you do, I am going to give you a trophy for your achievment, as this will make you a

true champion!

Surrender everything you have tied to or attached to your ego and lesser sense of self. As you surrender this part of yourself, your inner self will instantly fill the void, aligning you to a greater sense of oneness. It's like your spirit or soul is putting on a new garment, raising you up to higher levels. This is not an instant process but rather an ongoing one that happens daily in increments, similar to peeling back the layers of an onion.

Take a moment to consider how many years you've been living with your ego. It's as if we've woven a ball of yarn. Correcting ourselves takes time, and it may take some time to unravel it all, so be patient with yourself.

This part is truly liberating if you stick with me as we work on this together.

Surrendering the ego involves letting go of the need for control, validation, and constant self-importance. It's about transcending the limited sense of self that the ego represents and embracing a more expansive, interconnected way of being.

Keys to conquering your ego

- **Embody this book:** By being mindful and meditating, you will be quieter within, observing ego's patterns and reactions.
- **Practice humility:** Admit your mistakes, let them go, and focus on helping and serving others. Remember

sacrifice, surrender, selflessness, and service. Sacrifice and surrender yourself to become selfless in your actions of service to others.

· **Acknowledge the good deeds of others.** Doing so will enable you to grow and focus on their strengths instead of their weaknesses.

· **Start by telling yourself, "NO."** Self-discipline is crucial on this journey. Material possessions, unnecessary indulgences, or any external things that you believe will enhance your identity should be limited. Let's build our identity from within rather than relying on external factors.

· **Release any attachments you have.** Anything you rely on – whether it's your phone, your morning coffee, or even your loved ones – should be surrendered to your inner self. By this, I don't mean you should stop engaging in what you're doing; instead, you should let go of the self-desire attached to it, as this feeds the ego. By doing so, you can weave your inner self into the activity.

· **Keep concentrating on your breath.** Inhale the energy of the shining white pearl inside your heart, and nurture the fire of your heart as you exhale.

· **Keep your focus on your inner self, not your ego.** By embracing the inner self as your new reality, the shadows of the old self will gradually fade away. You are more likely to succeed if you have your inner self helping you.

· **Focus on the 'four pillars to oneness'.** Develop the habit of unconsciously practicing them, including 'listening gracefully', 'aligning yourself with nature', 'oneness in the shining white pearl', and 'constantly surrendering'.

· **Address this problem with love.** After reading this chapter, all you need to do is to examine this problem now with both the ego and love in mind. You know what needs to be done. I have laid out all the details for you. You are aware that you want to resolve it, and you understand that approaching the problem with a heart full of love will solve it. That's just the way it io.

"Nothing beats love!"

Now, imagine that you are a fly on the wall, observing the situation as if it were a chess game that you are about to play with yourself. Simply watch the moves it makes and laugh when it succeeds, which it might do from time to time. The first step is being aware and holding your desire to win. If you have that, you've already won.

Remember to stay present and composed, avoiding getting caught up in the past or fixating on the future. If you notice your ego trying to take over and attempting its defense mechanisms, acknowledge it.

Whisper softly to yourself:

"This is not happening."

Or, "No, I am not doing that."

Focusing on nurturing your inner child through creative expression can be helpful as well. The best way to counter a bossy tyrant ego is by becoming gentle and caring, and helping your inner child on their path being able to discern the difference between harshness and softness as they navigate with you through the changes you are making and can determine what truly matters.

When you notice your ego causing trouble, don't be too hard

on yourself. Instead, just smile and say, "Got ya!" Then, let go of the action and surrender your ego unto your higher self. If you do this every time you catch your ego in action, you'll speed up the process of you unravelling this ball of yarn and becoming your inner self.

Remember that the ego isn't essential for our survival; in fact, it's the main obstacle to our spiritual development. By releasing this part of ourselves, we don't disappear; instead, we become more aware of who we truly are.

The moments of clarity we reach during meditation can become a guide for our everyday lives as we maintain this constant connection. This also helps us become better individuals in our interactions with others, as the ego isn't constantly interfering for its own benefit. As we let go of our ego, our higher self replaces each layer, bringing us up higher to a more constant state similar to meditation.

"This is an ongoing but extremely rewarding process for those of you that choose to take on this challenge."

Meditation promotes a sense of unity

If you're not feeling the connection I'm talking about during your first time reading, which is the sense of being one with everything, I suggest focusing on meditation for the next two or three weeks. By practicing a ten-minute meditation daily for just two weeks, you'll notice significant changes within yourself. Meditation helps us break free from the feeling of separation from others. It brings us back to our natural state, allowing us to quickly recognize when thoughts and feelings begin to emerge and catch those subconscious influences that used to cause inner turmoil and busyness. Whenever you open your eyes after meditating for a few minutes, you'll find yourself in a heightened state of consciousness and more connected with everything.

It's time to expand

With the four pillars of oneness and overcoming the ego, we feel a greater sense of ease in stretching and expanding ourselves. We want to explore some simple ways to expand ourselves for fun.

Imagine breaking the concept of the coconut on your shoulder that limits your consciousness:

1. First, let's consider expanding through our breath. Practicing meditation by visualizing white fire tinged with golden-pink as we breathe out to the entire planet is a form of expansion. I haven't reached a point where I can do this continuously, but setting a five-minute timer on your phone and trying to operate throughout the day while breathing in that way until the alarm stops could be beneficial.
2. The experience of journeying through the shining white pearl in your heart is an intriguing thing to try. If you really want to expand, you can travel up the crystal cord to reach your secret star, which is the best way to go beyond the planet.
3. You can also enter the white fire pearl and see it expanding until you are within the pearl, then have it surround your property, house, and home. Stay at this level for a while

and focus on enveloping the area with love and charging it with light. Try increasing the intensity or even visualize brightening the individual atoms and electrons within your area. Once you feel comfortable, you can extend this exercise to include your city, country, and eventually the entire planet.

4. Imagine expanding a shining white pearl and traveling to a particular location to surround someone you love who needs comfort.

5. Envision expanding the shining white pearl to the size of the sun and travelling there. Place your shining white pearl on top of the sun, and its radiance will light and warm the planet.

6. Consider tracing your steps on the ground in the same way we send love from our hearts through our feet into the earth and connecting with the trees and bushes around you. What if you expanded your connection across the entire planet, completely connected with the whole planet and anchored with every tree at once?

7. Lastly, imagine expanding the shining white pearl within your heart to encompass the earth, allowing the same white fire and light within your heart to shine all across the planet. Fire that is invisible to the physical eye but can be seen on higher levels of consciousness, this is not a physical fire.

8. What if you could hold that white fire and light, spreading it all around the planet, then retreating back to the secret chamber of your heart where your shining white pearl and heart flame reside?

9. As you charge the fire on the pearl in your heart, it simultaneously lights up the planet around you on higher

levels as well.

10. What if with this new connection to mother nature and the earth, gave you the option to freely light up any region of the ground you wanted now?

11. You could even use the ground beneath someone sad or angry to comfort them, almost like giving them a hug without doing so physically.

If you could do even two or three of these numbered ideas here comfortably and effortlessly, you'd most defintely be in a different place to where you are now.

When I'm feeling energized and connected, these are some activities I love to do. Try them yourself to get your creative juices flowing. I'm sure you'll develop even more unique and magical ways to use your heart to help those around you.

Look at the stars at night

When we go about our day, we usually only look a few miles ahead, unless we're in an airplane, a tall building, or at a lookout. But at night, we can see tiny stars sparkling above us when the sky is dark. They are so far away that it makes me wonder how far we stretch our vision when we look at them.

This is the perfect time to explore expanding your focus and awareness of the world while being active.

You can pick a star in the sky and visualize entering the shining white pearl within the secret chamber of your heart. Then, visualize traveling to that star until the pearl envelops it and bringing the star back into your heart for expansion.

Alternatively, you can move from the first star to connect with another nearby star and start connecting the dots in the sky. After focusing on at least twenty different stars, open your vision and heart to all twenty-plus points at once. Visualize drawing all the stars into your heart to expand your consciousness.

Once you have expanded your awareness to this larger space, try seeing the white cloud of cosmic light substance and drawing it in to surround yourself or something else you are focusing on. You can also hold that connection with the multiple stars you are connected with and see if you can tune into their starlight and focus it into one point, such as yourself, something in front of you, or the ground below you.

Can the light within these stars be focused to help us in any way?

You will start asking and pondering These types of questions once you are more aligned and connected to everything. One of my most profound experiences is when you center yourself in your heart and start to see every cell of your body light up from its nucleus, shining with starlight. All the cells within your body start lighting up and shining at once. Then, visualize yourself opening up and the cells within your body becoming stars stretched throughout the cosmos. This brings you into a larger cosmic consciousness. I'll be leading you through a meditation on this at the end of the chapter - it's one of my absolute favorites.

Now, pause for a second and ask yourself, what is cosmic consciousness?

Listen to the souls of others when they speak to you

When speaking with others, focus on your heart, meaning the shining white pearl and your inner self. Keep your attention on these aspects as you converse with the other person.

As they speak to you, concentrate on the center of the shining white pearl within their hearts now, and listen to their words with love. Strive to listen gracefully, without letting your mind be filled with thoughts, hearing from the point within the shining white pearl in your heart and not your ears. Try to listen for their soul speaking to you beyond their words. It is your heart, not your mind that will be able to perceive it.

This gentle communication will either feel like gently spoken words within your heart or like a pure child speaking to you from the belly button or navel, where the soul often resides in others.

If you sense the other person's soul, let your love be like a rope and lift them up to the level of their inner self...

Just like my words are doing to you now;)

By practicing this, you will begin to light up the world for those around you. This is what we're chasing, isn't it?

This is part of the reason we are here: and that's to light up the world around us.

Reflection exercise: melt through every block in your body

For this next reflective exercise, similar to the chapter in which we explore dissolving the barriers within ourselves that prevent us from feeling connected to others, we will focus on the physical body, where many of us carry a lot of tension and blockages.

I want to take you through an exercise I learned during training in Wing Chun Kung Fu. This exercise has helped me release tension and open my body more in ways I didn't even realize were possible. It has helped me with becoming more mindful, and I hope it will do the same for you.

This exercise is different from the others. Please stand up straight and find an open space with enough room to stretch out your arms.

Stand with your feet shoulder-width apart. Take a few light steps to connect with the ground beneath you, similar to our previous grounding exercise.

Now, focus on your spine. Imagine a string pulling up from the top of your head, straightening and opening your spine slightly.

Take a few breaths to get comfortable. Direct your attention to the bottom of your spine, the tailbone or coccyx. Visualize a white pearl forming at the center of the base of your spine, similar to the white pearl in our hearts we've been visualizing. Breathe in white light from this pearl, drawing the air into your lungs. Hold the breath and then exhale, sending the air back down to the base of your spine, visualizing the light intensifying and dissolving any tension in that area. You may feel your hips rotate slightly, but just a tiny amount.

Now, we will work our way up each vertebra from the base of the spine to the skull. Visualize another sphere of white light forming between each vertebra, opening up the space between them until the sphere is the size of a ping-pong ball.

You should see two spheres of white light now, the one at the tailbone and the second on top of the tailbone between the two vertebrae.

We'll now repeat the process of seeing the next space between the next two vertebrae: seeing the white sphere form on top of the other two spheres and opening the space between the two vertebrae.

You can use your breath to help you release and open the space between the vertebrae. Breathe in to draw in any tension you are holding between the vertebrae, raising it up into the lungs, and breathe out to expand and open the space, seeing the white sphere expand to the size of a ping-pong ball

Remember to focus on each spine vertebra, visualizing a white sphere between every space. Start at the base of the spine and work your way up, opening and expanding each space between the vertebrae. You should see 33 white spheres in total, one for each vertebra. Continue raising and opening the spine until you reach the heart level, then move up to the neck and to the skull.

When you reach the skull, concentrate on the crown, visualizing a white sphere of light shining and expanding at the top of your head. Visualize the light from the base of the spine moving up to the crown of the skull. Use your breath as a guide, visualizing the light rising with each inhale.

Direct your attention to the top of the spine and imagine sending light down to fill the space of every vertebra down to the tailbone. If you struggle to visualize the white light, imagine a waterfall of white water filling each sphere like cups of light. This aligns and connects your spine.

Extend this alignment into your arms and legs. Picture two spheres forming under your armpits and in the space between your hips and groin, and visualize them opening up the joints. Inhale the tension and exhale, expanding the spheres in your shoulders and hips until they are the size of ping pong balls.

You can expand the white spheres in your hips and shoulders further or extend the light into your arms, visualizing it shining from your crown, down your spine, and filling your shoulders and hips. Continue until you feel the light filling your elbows and knees.

Repeat the process for your elbows and knees, visualizing spheres of light opening up these joints. Then, move on to your wrists and ankles, allowing the light to flow from your crown down through your spine into your arms, hips, and joints until you feel the wrists and ankles open.

Hold your focus on this for a little longer, seeing every joint open at once and breathing into it.

You have now built a circulatory system through your body, allowing you to transfer this mind force or chi from your crown through your hands and feet. Visualize the light flowing through your spine, hips, knees, and ankles into the ground beneath you.

Try to touch the forearm of your right arm with the fingertips of your left hand, transferring the light from your crown through your spine, shoulder, elbow, wrists, and into your forearm.

This exercise encourages integrating the senses with love. I encourage you to practice it until it becomes natural and automatic.

Optional extension: I recommend you give this next part at least once. We will scan through our body, using our fingertips to gently touch each part and release any muscle tension. While doing this, visualize the tension in your body as ice melting into water and then evaporating and dissipating into nothing.

Touch each part of your body slowly and softly for about two seconds, visualizing the tension melting away before moving on to the next area.

Here is the sequence to follow:

- Start by touching your eyebrows, the back of your head, the top of your head, your cheekbones, behind your ears, your jaw around where your wisdom teeth are, under your nose, between your bottom lip and chin, the back of your neck, each space within the vertebra down your neck.
- Then touch your collarbones, your shoulders, both of your triceps, biceps, elbows, the front and back of your forearms, and then your palms, and touch each joint in your thumbs and fingers.
- Move back to the body now and touch the top of your chest and the bottom of your ribs.
- Next, reach around to your lat muscles on your back and touch your spine, to your hips.
- Finally, touch your lower back, the front and top of your hips, buttocks, quads, hamstrings, knees, calves, ankles, and the spaces between every joint in your feet and toes.

This scanning process may initially take some time, but it can be done much faster in the future. After completing this exercise once, you may find it easier to open and feel each joint and part of your body the next time you run through the exercise.

It is up to you to decide whether this is due to us creating a new neural pathway within our minds or expanding our minds beyond our skull and into our joints.

After completing this exercise, you should feel relief in your body from releasing blocked energy. This detailed reflection may be long, but it is an important step to help you transfer your inner consciousness into the world around you.

Make sure to bring your focus to the shining white pearl within your heart and focus every joint and part of your body toward the shining white pearl and see all the light you have filled return into the shining white pearl.

Meditation exercise: cosmic consciousness

Close your eyes and slow down your thoughts and feelings as you enter a comfortable meditation state.

Use your breaths to draw everything in the world around you into your heart, making your heart the center of your focus.

See your heart shining now, shining like a sun. Golden white rays are shining, sending warm, inviting rays in all directions.

While focusing on your heart, you bring your attention to the sun itself and add its power and love into your heart, which you are sending out in all directions.

Now breathe in deeply, and as you breathe out, send your breath charged with your love in all directions like it is being sent out and following the golden white rays from your heart.

Once you feel centered and comfortable, see the cells within your body start to light up from the center of each cell with the same golden white light.

Wiggle your fingers and toes to help you see the added areas of cells in your body that will light up with this same golden white light until there are light pinpoints within every point of your body.

Seeing every pinpoint of light within every cell of your body, breathe in and out, this time seeing your breath as coming from the center of every cell in your body rather than just your lungs.

Every breath you take in connects you more to each cell of your body; every breath out makes them shine brighter and sends them further apart, increasing the space between each cell.

Take a deep breath, drawing in all your awareness to a single point within the center of your heart. See your heart explode, sending you up through your inner self, up through the secret star above you, and higher, sending you up in space.

Every pinpoint and cell within your body is now a star shining in space.

Your breath now becomes a force moving through space, and every cell of your body glows brighter and brighter with every breath you take.

You learn you can also move freely by focusing on one point and desiring to move there.

Listen deeply, what can you hear if you listen to the furthest reaches of space?

Can we bring every star around us into one point and re-launch ourselves into another dimension?

Or do we have the ability to align to every star within the cosmos and focus on one point bringing the light and energy into one area.

Spend as much time in this space as needed, enjoying the freedom you have, and make sure you remember this level of consciousness in the future.

Before you return to and open your eyes, make sure to bring in all the cells of your body you've stretched out through cosmos back to confines of your body.

Open your eyes again and take a moment to readjust yourself. You can journal your experience after finishing your experi-ence.

Things to consider

This reflective exercise was a long one, but I felt the need to include this in the book as it has been a step in my own personal journey to be able to not only transfer more light through my hands and feet into the world around me but also opening myself to where my body to become a vessel holding more light.

The earlier chapters on adding love to the sense of touch will help add another dimension of understanding to where you are now also transferring light. When I say light, I am referring to more of a spiritual energy which is a little higher in vibration to the lower physical planes, even though it can't always be seen. You can feel and sense when it is flowing through you.

After running through the exercise several times, you'll learn the majority of it from memory, and when you get out of bed and take your first step in the morning, you can simply pull the string from the top of your head to open your spine and spend a moment opening your spine with the ping pong visualizations or simply breathing in the energy of the tail of your spine to the level of your head and let it then flow down and fill your armpits, hips, elbows, knees, wrists and ankles with the light and start your day. You could also do this while you are standing in line waiting for a coffee, or making yourself a coffee, or while you're bored at work.

When we meditate, we clear our minds; this is doing the same thing for our spine and joints and body.

Once you run through the exercise of raising the light from the base to the skull once, it makes every future time a lot easier.

Once you are comfortable aligning yourself to this, one of the best feelings is when you begin to touch others say on their shoulder when they are down and sad. You witness a weight of sorrow lift off their shoulders.

This light atom meditation on cosmic consciousness where you extend your awareness throughout all of the cosmos always leaves me in a state of bliss. After doing it several times it makes it easy to enter into an active meditation when you are outside star gazing at night. Even while your walking conversing with someone, send yourself up there with all the stars, and see every star in the sky sending love and light to them as you talk, or if you are by yourself, extend yourself to be out with all the stars and look down at yourself on the outside looking in and send the love and light to yourself.

The most important part of this meditation, I will stress, is to make sure that when you close the meditation, you practice bringing all the stars in space into the confines of your body so that through constancy, you'll be able to open and close your cells more and more quickly, running through the process faster and opening yourself to more levels of consciousness.

14

Nature's Lessons: Finding Harmony in the World Around You

We have covered so much already. I want to dig deeper into nature, however. Nature is the key to becoming childlike and staying childlike.

Nature is so much fun.

I hold so many memories of finding this inner truth through nature. Like anything, though, it takes practice. After a while, though, every moment you are outside with nature, it feels like nature is singing to you.

Let us continue together as I share some more gems with you.

The spirit of nature

Before I go into depth with nature, the first thing to consider is to open our awareness to something beyond the physical involved here. I will refer to it as *'spirit'* as it seems like the most logical way to capture the magic of it without ruffling anyone's feathers.

Like in an earlier chapter where I was talking about the hidden magic present in the air we breathe, and how even though we can't physically see it, once we start acknowledging there is more than just air in the air we breathe is when the magic begins.

Have you noticed that for yourself yet?

If not, don't be scared to re-read that chapter again. This area is vital. Let us take the same approach as we ponder on the spirit that is present in nature.

Our physical body: the earth element

I touched lightly before on the elements of nature being congruent with the four quadrants of our being. Let us consider that the densest of our four bodies is Earth—the physical element.

We see the green in the trees and the green grass, flowers grown in perfect symmetry, and the earthy tones in the branches of the trees.

When we look at nature, we feel invigorated, as if there is a transfer of spirit to us when we look at nature.

We see the green and perfect colors, and it fills our body with a feeling of clarity and alignment. When you see trees or flowers, try to breathe in and accept the experience.

When you are more consciously aware of what is taking place when you look at nature, you will notice that transfer of spirit even more.

Once you have connected with what element of nature you're looking at, mirror that feeling within yourself that you're feeling from it in the same way I spoke of mirroring the sun.

Our emotional body: the water element

The water element is the same quadrant as our emotional body. Our emotional body is our feeling world. The feelings we feel in our solar plexus and the gut feeling we get are there to warn us about things. This is all tied in with our emotions, and the more intuitive we are with it, the more it works in our favour. It's funny how it soothes the soul when you hear rain on a tin roof, waves at the beach crashing on the sand, the sound of a waterfall, and even water dripping. The spirit in nature transfers through water to heal and realign our emotional body.

How good do you feel after a swim in the water?

I bet it feels even better when you're swimming at the beach.

Sometimes, I'm relaxing after an evening swim, and it's like I can still feel like I am rocking with the waves in the water.

When we drink water and give our body sustenance, there is a transfer of that spirit of life through the water into our emotions. If you're conscious of it, you'll feel it even better.

Any moment you're near water, let your inner child be free. You can absorb the gift of water even if you look at it or listen to the sound of it dancing (or moving); if you do this while loving your emotional body and yourself, you'll feel that transfer too.

You can also experiment with mirroring the water with your emotions, providing it's a large area of clean and fresh water, like the beach or a river.

Our mental body: the air element

The air and wind are one with our minds.

If you are driving at night and are nodding off, wind down

the window and let some fresh air wake you up quickly. Fresh air clears and fills the mind, primarily when breathing through our nose, bypassing the brain.

The air and wind around us transfers that spirit of life to us through our breath.

If you are mindful of this happening when you breathe, you'll quickly be alert, awake, and clear-minded. It's hard to have negative thoughts when you breathe in this spirit of life. It is healing in so many ways.

Whenever it is windy, whistle to the wind; in this way, you are in harmony with nature and creating music to nature's tune. You'll see the relationship you build with nature makes this journey much more fun.

With those **22,000** breaths daily, the air element is close and with us always.

Our memory body: the fire element

Our memory or etheric body is in the same quadrant as the fire element—the highest in the vibration of the four. We don't often see fire, but when we sit in front of a fire, we feel like memories are being consumed.

Everything is consumed and returned to the source by the spirit of fire.

The family fire in the living room was the TV set for families before the TV was invented. The yellow-orange light is also perfect for helping us produce melatonin to help us wind down at night before sleeping.

As fire is the highest in the vibration of the elements, we can use the visualization of fire with our meditations, especially when faced with consuming memories of pain.

I meditate with the violet flame surrounding me daily and have found it an incredible tool to help me work through removing many burdens from me, burdens I didn't even realize I was carrying.

Reflection exercise: tracing the roots

Take a second to go outside and connect with nature.

You are looking at the trees and surroundings with love.

Acknowledge the spirit of life being transferred to you, then breathe it in. Your physical body and mental body are recharging simultaneously. Thank your heart for the experience and mirror what you see.

- If there is a tree in reach, go up and touch it.
- Rest your palm and lean on it, sending love through your hands.
- Try to sense the tree with your feeling world.
- Send love from your heart into the tree, down to the roots, and into the Earth.

From there, feel any other plants in sight connected to you on the Earth in the same way.

Stretch your awareness into the world, touching every single plant earthed with its roots in the ground on the planet.

Thank them for their service, and send them love. Now, find a peaceful and quiet place to sit in the area with nature and absorb your experience and connection with nature.

You may journal your thoughts if you feel prompted.

Meditation exercise: finding mother nature

Like the reflective exercise in this chapter, let us go outside and attune to nature. Sit and get yourself comfortable looking and listening with an empty mind.

Acknowledge the spirit of life being transferred to you through what you see. Listen to the sounds with all the love in your heart, breathe deeply through your nose, feel the spirit of life fill your mind and body, and then breathe out.

Breathe again through your nose, closing your eyes and centering in your heart.

Rest your hands palms down on the ground, either next to you as you're sitting or leaning forward so you are touching the ground in front of you.

Send love through your hands into the Earth.

See the shining white pearl in your heart become the sphere your hands are resting on. This is the Divine Mother or Mother Nature. Send love through your hands to her.

Breathe in and out, whispering, *"I AM forgiving the divine mother completely."*

Breathe in and out, reciting the affirmation again, *"I AM forgiving the Divine Mother completely."*

Repeat this nine times, then see yourself surrounded by white fire coming from the ground below you. See it burning in through the whole planet, transmuting all hatred and anger worldwide—hatred within the people and hatred towards the Divine Mother.

That shining white pearl within your heart, you learn, is the Divine Mother. This is your point and connection to the planet as a whole. This is where the spirit meets the physical, and it is all within the heart of your being.

Now open your eyes and return to, still seeing the white fire if you can.

This fire is the fire of the Mother.

Stand up when you are ready. And step, seeing and feeling the white fire rise from the ground when you step. You still see the shining white pearl within your heart glowing with the same white light as the Earth beneath you. Look at nature, seeing the white fire burning around and through it.

Is this what it looks like on higher octaves of consciousness? Time will tell.

You now have a new understanding and connection with nature.

Treasure and nurture it all the way until the end of your meditation and beyond.

Things to consider

Tracing the roots helps ground us even deeper and enter into a oneness with nature. The more we give this exercise, the more you'll feel a connection with every plant in sight at once. You'll also be able to trace into the heart of the Earth, sending love from the heart to bless the world around you and receiving love back from the Earth in return.

This meditation exercise on connecting to the Divine Mother or Mother Nature will bring a new sense of oneness into your world. During the visualization where I mentioned seeing the white fire around you, if you can't see it, don't force it, feel it. This white fire gives you a true tone when you know the ground beneath you.

If you begin to look at nature and see the white within what you are looking at, this will also help you find and give you a stronger connection. If you practice this meditation more while sitting, you can see the white fire around you consuming all with your eyes closed. In time, you may continue to see it even after you open your eyes.

15

Healing the Past: Letting Go of Painful Memories

Sitting in meditation for long periods with your mind stilled and at peace is a part of the physiological process for past painful memories to surface from the subconscious into the conscious mind for us to face again, deal with, and let go.

With the correct methodology to handle this, we can witness the release of shackles holding down our souls. As this pain transmutes, we feel liberated and lighter as a person with a new lens in how we view the world.

Similar to when speaking with a psychologist and memories surface in your mind, and we talk them out and come to an inner resolution, we may also have a similar experience in meditation if you can learn to forgive and let it go when it surfaces.

Disclaimer alert

I am not saying this meditation approach should replace therapy or any medical treatment you currently are on. Meditation will serve to help in conjunction with what you are already doing.

This chapter here focuses on an easier handling of the process should it surface. I have to make this clear so that both of us are protected.

What is going on?

Any traumatic memory or negative emotions we hold towards others or ourselves, often rather than looking at it square in the face in front of us, we burrow it down, pushing it down to deal with later. The problem is that we don't end up dealing with it, and our patterns in life either repeat themselves or we have other negative feelings we focus on to mask that pain.

With our eyes closed, we look into our subconscious.

That's why it is difficult for many people to close their eyes comfortably, and as we still our thoughts and feelings kindling the flame of love within our hearts, that flame intensifies daily.

Think of a pot of water on the stove; as the flame increases, the heat of the water, the water (like the water of our emotional body) begins to bubble, and things start to come to the top and surface that we may have forgotten about. The key is not to be attached, to observe what is going on, and to let it evaporate into nothing.

What is processing?

To understand what is going on here as this is happening, let us call the whole process of what is going on 'processing'. Think of yourself like a hot air balloon; the flame in your heart increases in heat, increasing your consciousness. However, it can't raise up in height if you are still attached to this pain on lower levels, so it surfaces for your soul to resolve where you can forgive yourself or others completely. The pain attached to that moment fades away, and your soul can soar to a higher level.

Let us drop the sand bags holding us down and go up higher.

Forgive both yourself and others

The greatest virtue of love is being able to forgive others. While you may not be able to forgive the crime or action, you can still forgive the person's soul. The wisest words on forgiveness I've heard were Gautama Buddha's words when he said, *"Holding onto anger is like drinking poison and expecting the other person to die."*

Nobody wants to poison themselves, do they?

Yet we do it unknowingly when we hold onto things we or others have done to us that are karmically holding us down and preventing us from moving forward.

One of my greatest teachers on forgiveness has been my Mother. I wasn't aware at the time in my younger years, but through all our ups and downs growing up the following day, she would always forgive me as if nothing had happened.

This is true love. Knowing that all of us are here making mistakes in life to learn what to do right the next time we face a similar situation. No one can truly understand what someone is going through within themselves when they are acting and doing something wrong.

- *Would we have made a different choice if we were put in their situation?*

265

We may be learning lessons in life dealing with being on the receiving end of the actions of others: these are our tests of how far we have come or how far we still need to go.

Forgive yourself

When you condemn yourself, you immediately take yourself outside the circle of oneness. I said it earlier in the book and I'll say it again. Repetition equals retention, and I want you to remember this. We all walk through life learning from our rights and wrongs; nonetheless, often, we can be wrestling within ourselves, beating ourselves up for all the horrible things we may have done in life.

The fact is, as soon as our head hits the pillow at night, we wake up the next day a new person with the opportunity to make things right and to live our life again in trying to be a better person.

Some of you reading or listening to this may not be able to do this, but that's okay.

The more we still our minds and bring our thoughts and feelings into alignment, the more you may find yourself going through this processing phase.

Until then, let us keep improving ourselves gradually until we can look back on ourselves to who we were months or even years ago with a shining smile, knowing you are not the same person you were at that time, just as you are not the same person you were yesterday. We are constantly changing and evolving to become better people, but if you want to be the person you were yesterday, that's all you will be.

Make your *choice*; the only person who can change this is *you*.

Surrender, let go, forgive, then love

Whenever life gets too much, we must learn to surrender.

By surrendering, we lose the sense of struggle.

We don't even know the meaning of the word.

By truly surrendering, we let go of the issue and forgive ourselves and all those attached to what we were focusing on, sending love into the situation no matter how hard it feels to do.

If you find yourself struggling to let go of something or surrender, I suggest you experiment with the violet flame.

See a pillar of violet flame in and around yourself as you are processing, and the flames are burning away the memories and the negative feelings that are holding on.

Let it build in layers of strength around your heart and spread all through your body, and let the visualization of this fire help you consume and transmute those negative memories and records that are being cleared right before your very eyes.

How to forgive with love

Like the exercise in an earlier chapter where I showed the virtue of peace flowing from the solar plexus as an extension of love, let us go through the ritual of forgiveness together.

Feel that feeling of love filling your heart and extend down into the level of your belly button.

This is the area of your subconscious.

Love flows from your heart, filling the area of your belly button and extending out into your world in a true tone of violet, which is the tone of mercy and forgiveness.

Rather than seeing the waters flowing from the solar plexus

like we did before, we now see a violet fire burning deeply within us.

- We see it burning away at every part of ourselves until things start surfacing.
- We see pictures of the memories being transmuted and the feelings tied to that moment being released from us.
- The perfect tone of violet helps us to let go of everything and just observe the process.

Violet fire builds around us and intensifies as orbs containing concentrated balls of violet fire start to fly out in every direction from our belly button and out into the world to those who are tied to the memories surfacing.

The violet flame helps us let go, and at the same time, the balls of fire being sent to the people connected to those memories help them to let go as well.

Burdens are lifted off and released from you as you feel the painful memory being erased. This process lifts us up and helps bring us closer to a new sense of alignment.

Fear is not real

Every negative emotion we feel stems from fear and doubt.

When confronting anger or hatred, look at the fear behind the problem. Once you clear the fear, the momentum of the other emotions will be erased much more quickly.

It is essential to know that fears often go back to childhood, and even though the memories of fear were at the age of an adult, those feelings of fear are linked back to when you were young.

268

I suggest you rest your hands on your lap and imagine you are cradling the child version of yourself; call it your inner child, if you will and comfort them with love. You can speak to it as you process to help them let go, for we must let go to go higher.

Raising attainment

As we start to do the work within ourselves in resolving these personal burdens within ourselves, once we feel the weight lift off our shoulders from the baggage we didn't even realize how much was holding us down, we become hooked.

You feel lighter, you feel clearer, and your soul feels free. You look at yourself, realizing how much more work there is to do.

You then can start picking the negative emotions or habits you desire no longer to have within yourself or engage with them, and then work day by day picking out the weeds in the garden of your being, to the point in which you begin to walk the world completely free of jealousy, for example, happy in others' success, or completely fearless, never wrestling with anxiety again, knowing that the feeling you previously labeled as fear is your body telling you, *"Yay, let's do this. I am excited about taking the next step forward to conquering this."*

Reflective exercise: write a letter on forgiveness

I want you to get a pen and paper for this reflective exercise and write notes. Be honest with yourself through this; no one will read this but you. At the top of the page, I want you to write, *'I call on the law of forgiveness and forgive completely...'* and then start writing.

Start with your partner or previous partner, and trace back your relationships, then your mum and dad, siblings, room-mates, friends, old friends you may no longer be in touch with, old work colleagues and boss; keep writing.

Even people that have passed on and are no longer in em-bodiment. Once you get momentum in your writing, you'll feel stuff surface, but keep writing and flowing with it.

Go to every person or thing you can remember, and then I want you to finish by forgiving yourself.

Anything you have ever beaten yourself up for doing, write on paper, *'I forgive myself for doing ..... so many years ago...'.*

Forgiving yourself is the hardest part of letting go, but you will feel a shift once you do. This may be a short exercise, or you may keep writing for pages.

Once you finish this exercise, find a lighter or a box of matches. I ask you now burn this letter and let these memories go forever.

Once it is burnt, you are entirely free from holding onto it.

As you light it and watch the flames consume it, say to yourself, *"I AM forgiving everyone mentioned in this letter, and call on the law of forgiveness."*

I call it a law because that is what it is; once we forgive someone or something, it liberates us from it.

Re-read the chapter above, *'How to forgive with love'*, and run through this ritual if needed. If you follow this exercise I have given, I promise you with all my heart you will benefit greatly.

Meditation exercise: meditation on the violet flame

For this meditation, sit upright and get comfortable, centering all your energies to enter into the shining white pearl within your heart.

Start by visualizing the fire within your heart, then let the flame turn to violet, burning in the heart and surrounding the heart, watching the violet flame increase in size, encompassing the physical heart.

Focus on the flame and your breathing as you are fanning the flame. Let it expand slowly so that it appears so thick and intense that you cannot see through it.

See the flame increase and fill your neck, throat, and mind, clearing your vision completely.

Now visualize the violet flame rising from beneath your feet, rising and pulsating and purifying every part of your being.

When you can see and feel it filling every part of your body, let it extend out from you slowly, like you have an aura filled with violet flame, gradually increasing and intensifying to where you can expand your awareness beyond the area of your house and home, your city, and eventually the planet.

From here, you can meditate on the flame itself, letting it intensify with every breath you take, or meditate on moments in your life where resolution is needed.

- See the scenes or memories that surface in your mind and see the violet flame consuming them completely.
- You may wish to think of a particular person you have hurt or someone who previously hurt you. See the violet flame, freeing you both from whatever has happened. See it melting away all pain.
- See it fill your heart and their heart, dissolving all ties you have to them.
- If you see the memories of any event surface, breathe in,

accept, and breathe it out, letting it go, letting the plumes of the flame dissolve the memory forever.

- If the memories or moments get too intense, step back within yourself, focus on your heart and love yourself, resting your palms on your lap face up and cradle and comfort your inner child through it
- Once you feel the liberation from a resolution from one person or event, you may move to another person and work through everyone you can think of to free you both. You can then trace back through memories dating back to your childhood.

The more you practice this ritual, the more you will begin to see every small part of your psyche resolved by using the violet flame, which is a flame of forgiveness.

Things to consider

If you partake in this reflection exercise, you will benefit immensely. It may seem intrusive for me to ask this of you, and if it does, I do apologize.

Once you take the first step in facing yourself and letting it out on paper and then burning it after, letting it dissolve from your world, there is an alchemy to this.

I often write letters and burn them, asking for help on various issues in my life.

This ritual has great healing; I encourage you to try it at least once. No one will be reading it but you, and that is only to prepare you to let it go into the flame so you can feel a new sense of peace within yourself and continue to be a better and bigger person and be of greater service to life.

This meditation on the flame of forgiveness is an incredible ritual. Once you feel the joy in the violet flame around you, you can add this visualization of this violet flame into every meditation I have shared with you in earlier chapters. You can even work towards opening your eyes and holding the visualization while your eyes are open.

If someone is angry at you, send them violet flame. Use the violet flame if you are angry at someone else. With consistent use of the violet flame, I find it hard to stay angry at someone for more than a day now. If you bring this reflective technique into your daily life, you will see immense changes happening for the better.

The greatest gift of the violet flame though, is that it helps your soul infuse with your inner self. Every time you practice using the violet flame, your soul is infusing with her inner self. At the same time, your inner self is infusing with your soul.

16

Next Steps: Your Journey Beyond Meditation

So, we are coming closer to the book's conclusion now, but there are a few more keys I would like to share to anchor the change that has occurred within you.

Whether you are religious, spiritual, or both, or have read or listened to this to get a deeper connection to life, every single path to life shares one common goal: to be the best version of ourselves.

Every day moving forward, we get to try again and do it a little bit better. We can take a curious stance towards experimenting with what works in our life by running with something if it works and then dropping it if it doesn't.

The key is to keep everything fresh and look to life like you never stop learning; you are always growing, and look at the goal of having a perfect life as being a sequence of perfect days.

Every day, if you can lay your head on the pillow at night, looking back on the day not being able to critique yourself about your actions that day, then you know you can drift off to sleep and know you are heading in the right direction.

The greatest joy in life though, is knowing when you wake up the next morning, you get a chance to do it all again, only better and with a greater sense of love and a greater sense of victory.

Getting to this level of living life is what I am striving for; I will talk about this more in books to come.

Let your heart become a magnet

Let your heart become a magnet. *'Nothing But Love'* should be your motto. Any situation, interaction, or reaction, before you act, recite in your heart nothing but love and then fuel the whole situation or problem with love.

People will see it, even if they may not understand it—*'Nothing But Love."*

With constancy in putting love behind your senses, practicing these meditations and exercises with the sun and nature, you will put love into everything you do.

Even the simplest moments of life will give you the greatest surges of joy as your heartbeat dances like a metronome to the cycles of life, which can be heard and felt throughout the cosmos.

I am stretching your vision to show you that there is no limit to where you can take these pearls of wisdom I have shared.

Give me one month

If you've been listening to this book while driving or reading through it, and although some of my words have made sense, some may sound a little far-fetched...

"He said to touch the trees and trace the roots into the ground?"

"He wants us to breathe out across the whole planet?"

"What do you mean stretch our cells to become the stars through-out all of the cosmos?? Man! This guy is cooked!"

I'll take that **100%** and know, though what I am saying is out there and could be seen as crazy, but do you know what? Can you honestly say that throughout your whole life, in every year you've been on this planet, you've felt complete?

There has got to be more to life than being a slave to society for the prime years of our lives just for a handful of temporary moments of stimulation in the outer events around us.

Give me one month to practice what I have shared.

What have you got to lose?

Even if you quit after that month, your life, for what you know it, will never be the same.

You will be brighter, lighter, and more full of life.

Please review the book, pick four or five things you like, and practice them daily. Please keep it to yourself; no one needs to know but you. Then you can honestly say to yourself, okay, I tried it, and it's bonkers and not for me.

If you have been reading this book and completing the reflections and meditations, that is incredible, and I am extremely proud of you. There are different levels of consciousness for us to explore if we focus on these concepts with constancy.

I suggest you scroll through the book and write down all the things you want to try and squeeze into your days. Time block it: meaning, have a list of every line being an hour of the day, and realistically, with your life, try to slot in several exercises or moments throughout the day in your daily schedule. Try putting the sheet somewhere you can see in the morning before you start your day and somewhere you can see towards the end of the day.

With the reflections and meditations, re-read them before you go through them again so they are fresh in your mind. Then, when you actively practice these techniques, you will retain the information and knowledge of how to do these to where the meditations and reflections will become yours that you can see clearly by memory, giving you something to add to your life as you continue your journey by yourself.

I am still with you, though, in heart, and I encourage you to pick up the book and re-read it if you ever feel like you're slowing down in progress and want to pick up your energy and commit again.

Speak from the heart and not the ego

You may not be able to sense this immediately, but I have been prompted to share this with you. And that is, the more we become heart-centered and walk through life qualifying all of our actions with love, we will start to accumulate more love and light within our being.

Like the spirit that we see and feel in our breath, we become a vessel holding more of that light. You'll notice that you'll come to a point where talking with others can drag you back down.

The majority of the world speaks from the level of the ego, which is the lesser self.

I'm not saying that you are an egoless being just yet, I am saying because you are speaking from the level of the heart, you'll feel when you are centered at the level of the heart, and you speak from there to the other person's heart, you'll bring light into any given situation, but not misqualify energy.

Be mindful, though, when you speak with someone, it may

feel like their words are coming from the level of their gut; we don't want to speak to that; we want to speak to their heart.

The count to three is your greatest tool of defense, or the nothing-but-love approach, which takes three seconds to whisper to yourself and serves the same purpose.

So when words are darted to you from below the heart, you can absorb them, smile, and speak back at the heart-to-heart level.

Teach others with love

Until you have developed a solid link to speaking from the inner levels of your being that I told of in earlier chapters, be humble and keep your internal changes in alchemy.

The greatest gift we can give the world is love.

When you listen to people, and you listen with love, you open their hearts to that flame through your interaction.

When you ask them questions about what they are going through, they will feel that love you are transferring to them. And if you speak to their heart and not their ego, you'll lift them.

Only advise others if they ask for advice.

Half the time, people already know the answer; if you lead them, you are not enabling them to find the answer themselves.

It takes practice, but when you get good at it, it becomes effortless, and you have no human will tied up in their problems. To give you an idea, lead them with open questions like:

"Okay, have you weighed up all your options?"

Then... *"Out of those, which one do you feel is the right way for you?"*

Nine times out of ten, they will answer it for themselves,

which will be a win-win for both of you.

Re-read this book until you become it

Rome wasn't built in a day, and even if you have put 100% effort into this book with all the reflections and meditations, and daily practicing the suggestions I have given, you would have seen a massive shift in your world, but there still is a lot of work to do.

We are plucking out momentums and habits that have been active for years. Let's go through the book again in three to six months.

You may not have to participate in every exercise through the chapters, but think of going back to the campfire to unlock another layer of the puzzle until you listen and hear the final keys, where you can continue your life for yourself.

Some of you may only need to listen to it once, as everyone is different.

Embody gratitude

Gratitude is becoming increasingly recognized in science and health as one of the greatest virtues to practice to counter things such as depression. Remember when I spoke of four or five things you love doing?

Take some time out at least once and write down a list of all the things you are grateful for.

That list then becomes like a rudder to your boat to help you shift away from the storms as you sail through life.

The more you start practicing acknowledging gratitude, the more you build momentum with it.

To give you an example, I started writing down in my journal five things I was grateful for every night for two or three months, and then I was conversing with one of my siblings about someone they were being negative about. I just started speaking about that person, and the most beautiful words flowed out of my mouth, speaking so highly of them.

The only way I can explain what I experienced from my end was like golden water bubbling up from my belly to my heart.

I firmly believe in my heart of hearts; those nights of writing down nightly five lines of five things I am grateful for, I was feeding positive energy into my subconscious, which surfaced at a time when I needed it.

Embody joy

With everything I have shared in this book, joy is the greatest virtue you can cultivate. Have fun with it. Who cares what anyone else says to you? You can waste your whole life trying to impress other people. If something feels like it would be fun to do, then be a kid.

Take your shoes off and step in the water.

Climb the tree in the park, even if there are people around.

What else is there to do if you are child-hearted, keep it simple, and love the world and the things you do with constancy?

Reflection exercise: attune your inner ear

For this reflective exercise, I want to show you how to develop your inner ear more.

I want you to jump on YouTube and search for "321 Relaxing

– Meditation Relax Clips", it is a channel with a lot of different music, not all of it is sleeping music, but find something you enjoy or a song of similar nature, buddha flutes, piano, hang drum, hand pan, or something along those lines and listen to it with grace.

This is an active meditation.

You are breathing in and emptying your mind, listening to the sounds, not with your ears, from your heart. Love the music, and start searching for ways to listen to it in and with your heart. Can you hear the instruments playing in your heart, like each note bumps you softly?

Keep listening and enter a deeper state of grace, absorbing everything you hear with love.

Meditation exercise: the flame of illumination

For this meditation, it is better to be seated.

We want to close our eyes, stilling our thoughts and feelings to enter into that emptiness of peace. If any thought surfaces, accept it and let it pass.

First, we will enter into the secret chamber within our hearts, seeing the flame burning from the shining white pearl within our being.

We see yellow flames burn through our minds and fill our heads.

The yellow is radiant and vibrant, like the color of daisies or canola oil flowers.

You feel it expand and intensify through the top of your skull until it widens and surrounds you, burning like a pillar of fire extending two feet above you.

- All density within you is consumed.
- Your mind expands and is free.
- You feel a oneness with your inner self.
- You feel aware of your true identity as your mind lifts above you.

Stay at this height of the inner recesses of your being and enjoy remembering and retaining the state of consciousness you strive for. When the time is right, open your eyes again. Thank your heart flame for the experience. You may journal any insights should you feel prompted.

Things to consider

Once cultivated, this reflective exercise of attuning to your inner ear will give you the gift of being able to listen from a higher level of consciousness. Like the meditation we gave in trying to speak from that inner level of consciousness, this is helping us to hear from that same place.

When listening, we bring that level of consciousness into the physical world around us. This is the ultimate goal in raising attainment, that is, to bring those inner levels we reach in our hearts into the physical world around us.

The meditation on the flame of illumination is a great one to give before studying, working, or when you need an answer. You can also give it when hitting a block in any level of your being.

Practicing using the flame of the illumination is not to be missed, and even seeing it around you for two to three minutes daily will help you to see through, giving you insight into how to overcome even the most difficult of circumstances.

17

Final Words: Embracing Your New Life Path

I hope you have found my words to hold your interest, inspire and entertain you, and you have taken something away from them. I have spent years trying to find what works for me, and this is my story, but what is yours?

Hopefully, this book has saved you a lot of time picking and choosing what you want to integrate into your life. You may decide to swing in a completely different direction, and that's completely fine, as you are a creature of free will. I have put much thought into sharing this message and transferring what I've learnt over the years onto you.

The goal of any teacher is to do their best to simplify it so that those they share their wisdom with can grasp it even quicker and more accessible and hopefully even exceed the teacher in time if the teacher has done their job right.

There is a lot of content here to experiment with and see what works for you and what doesn't. Meditation can bring so much joy into your life if you practice it daily. Not just closed eyes but listening and functioning in the world with an empty mind. The less you think, the more you'll see the world for what it is, not blinded by your perspective.

This is my first book. It's the first of more to come. I love writing. It flows from the heart. When you write from the heart, you fill the words with love like they have been charged with light and come from a good space.

Please leave me a review if you have a moment. It means the world to my book sales as people will often look to the reviews as being the decision makers if they are torn between two books. Even if what you have read or heard is far-fetched or too out there for you, please give your review for the effort and amount of content I have provided. This is a sensitive topic that often ruffles a lot of feathers.

I thank you for sticking with me until the end and hope to see you find this magical world that I have found by searching for a deeper connection to life.

I wish you all the best on your journey in life and promise you that you will get even more from my book the second time if you choose to pick it up again. Please remember that the next time you see the cover before you.

Yours Truly,

David

Made in the USA
Columbia, SC
31 July 2024

39681814R00161